MONEY
MANAGEMENT
WISDOM
for
MILLENNIALS

MMW

Money Management Wisdom

by MERRIE ALLMON ALLEN

Money Management Wisdom for Millennials
Copyright © 2017 by Merrie Allmon Allen

Scripture quotations have been listed at the end of the book.

FIRST EDITION

Published by
DANKEI PUBLISHING

www.MoneyManagementWisdom.net

merriebay@gmail.com

Library of Congress Cataloging-in-Publication Data

ISBN: 978-0-692-84755-8

1. Personal Finance. 2. Faith.

2017910674

Foreword by Dr. Samuel Maxwell

Format by Eli Blyden | www.EliTheBookGuy.com

Dedication

In loving memory of my mother, Mae F. Bonner Allmon
A woman who was smarter than she ever realized
who could have been anything she wanted
who graciously navigated the life
she was given
including
loving
me

Foreword

Only a few pastors get the privilege of writing the foreword in a book written by someone who grew in grace under their leadership. Merrie Allmon Allen has afforded me the opportunity to enjoy such a distinguished privilege. She connected with our church in 1997, only three years after I accepted the call to pastor the First Baptist Church of Progress Village. Merrie has not only grown and matured over the years, but has been instrumental in the growth and development of this ministry. *Money Management Wisdom for Millennials* is, in fact, a direct result of the author's commitment to teaching Young Adult Sunday morning Bible Study.

Benjamin Franklin is often quoted as having said, "Experience is the best teacher. . ." However, few people are aware that there's more to the quote. Franklin continues by saying, ". . . but a fool will learn from no other." I'm sure that many baby boomers, my generation, would agree that life would have been more spiritually prosperous if the wisdom of this work had been available during our young adult lives.

Solomon writes, "Wisdom crieth without; she uttereth her voice in the streets. . ." (Proverbs 1:20). Merrie also cries out to millennials with the wisdom of Solomon, her vocational skills, and her faith experience with God and money. I encourage young adults, and all believers, to learn the lessons of wisdom so as not to repeat the mistakes of the past concerning money management.

– Dr. Samuel Maxwell
Senior Teaching Pastor
First Baptist Church of Progress Village
Tampa, Florida

Acknowledgements

Ricky Allen. Your patience with me and all things Merrie is amazing and so very much appreciated. I promise that the late-night-early-morning writing is over for a while. I'm looking forward to getting back to speaking your love language of quality time.

Danielle and Keith Bayard. You are my inspiration and the reason I do what I do. Wanting the best for you is what drives me to want the best for other young adults. I've learned so much about love, life, and sacrifice simply by being your mom. I love you guys.

Samantha Hill, Captain, USAF. My millennial goddaughter who gives me great insight into the millennial mindset. I love our "debates" even when you're pointing out my short-sightedness.

Walter Allmon, Carol Allmon Watts, Robert Watts, Mark Allmon, Kelly Jones, Brittany Allmon, and Brandon Allmon— my family. Through the good, bad, and utterly insane, we manage to love just the same. Thank you.

Yolanda Killings, Fabiola Mehu, Wendy Johnson, Joyce Stokes, Kelly Alexander and Yolanda Cole. Your support over the years has been tremendous. Thank you for encouraging me, being a listening ear, and providing years of laughter and good times. Wendy--you have no idea how much I appreciate your taking the time to help with this project.

Rob Wilson of Rflatsolutions.com. My "little brother" and very good friend. Look how far our kitchen table conversation has come. Thank you for pushing me through the process, holding me accountable, and creating my fabulous website. You rock!

Jorgie Franks-Bell, www.jorgiefranks.com and Eli Blyden, www.EliTheBookGuy.com. Thank you for sharing your expert knowledge of the self-publishing process. It seems you have sparked my newest passion. Book number two has already been outlined.

Accounts payable millennials of Hillsborough County Clerk of Courts, County Finance. You guys give me hope in your generation by defying the negative stereotypes. Thank you for bringing your "A" game every day.

Tauchante McCullum and Kayla Redmond, my dynamic duo millennial review team. Thanks for reading my manuscript and your honest feedback. I've already booked you for my next project.

First Baptist Church of Progress Village. Pastor Maxwell, thank you for being my pastor, teacher, and friend and for the privilege of serving under your leadership. To the youth and young adults, thank you for allowing me to walk in my purpose. Through exercising my gifts of teaching and mentoring, I pray I've made a small impact on your lives. You've certainly made an enormous impact on mine.

Most importantly, to my Lord and Savior Jesus Christ; thank you for continuously blessing me far beyond what I deserve. My sincerest desire is to honor you with this project. My prayer is that young adult lives are changed as they learn to properly manage their precious gifts of time, talent, and treasure.

Getting the Most from This Book

To get the most from this book, I suggest you follow up with the references. The articles and other resources contain a wealth of relevant information that I think you will find very useful.

The scriptures are identified by quoted, *italicized* text, and the scripture references are listed in the back of the book. Some individuals may prefer to read the book and review the scriptures later; others may pause and read the scriptures as they go along. Either way, I suggest that you also read a few scriptures from the Bible that fall before and after the focus scripture. This will help you better understand the context. Some of the scriptures may not directly reference money or possessions, but rather highlight a principle to be applied to the management of your finances.

Lastly, be sure to answer the questions at the end of each chapter. The questions are designed to encourage you to reflect on how you're currently handling your money and what you could be doing better. Once you've completed the book, visit my website, **www.moneymanagementwisdom.net,** or my Facebook page @Money Management Wisdom for Millennials, and provide feedback or ask a personal finance question. I'd love to hear from you!

Table of Contents

MONEY MANAGEMENT WISDOM for MILLENNIALS

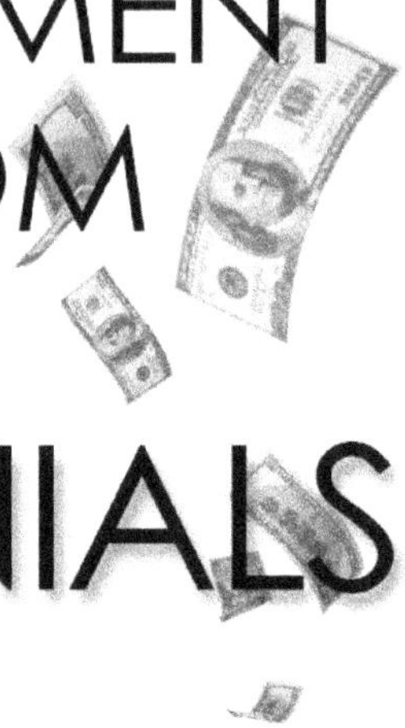

The Case for Wisdom

Blessed is the one who finds wisdom, and the one who gets understanding. (Proverbs 3:13)

A young man was newly appointed king of a great nation. Governing a nation was not going to be an easy task. After all, the job involved dealing with the personalities, attitudes, and concerns of many people. He was smart enough to know that given his inexperience and the large task ahead, he would need help to be successful. God gave the man an opportunity to ask Him anything his heart desired. Of all the things in the world the man could ask for, Solomon responded, *"Give me now wisdom and knowledge to go out and come in before this people, for who can govern this people of yours, which is so great."*[a] Solomon asked for wisdom and understanding so that he would be able to rule the people justly and make good decisions on their behalf. And, because Solomon did not selfishly ask for riches or fame, God granted both. He became the wisest, wealthiest, and most popular man of influence in all the land. People came from far and near to partake of his wisdom.

This story illustrates the high value placed on wisdom. A simple Google search defines wisdom as the quality of having experience, knowledge, and good judgment. King Solomon advises, *"Wisdom is the principal thing; therefore get wisdom: and with all thy getting get understanding."[b]* To successfully manage your money, you need knowledge, wisdom, and understanding.

Knowledge is simply facts or information. Your credit card issuer is charging you an APR of 18%. That is a fact.

Understanding is being able to apply meaning to the fact. If you have a balance of $1,200 on your credit card and pay the monthly minimum of $30, it will take you 62 months to pay off the balance, and you will have paid $647 in interest—the additional cost of your $1,200 purchases. You understand the effects of the fact.

Wisdom is knowing how to apply your knowledge and understanding based on your values and desired outcome. If you desire to minimize the amount of time you remain in debt and pay the least amount of money, wisdom will tell you to increase your monthly payment. Increasing your monthly payment to $100 will take only 14 months and cost $133 in interest to get rid of this debt. Can you see how using wisdom in making financial decisions can make an enormous difference?

I wrote *Money Management Wisdom for Millennials* to educate, inspire, and provide you practical ways to manage your money. You will learn how to stop living paycheck to paycheck, create a plan for getting out of debt, and prepare for future financial success and worry-free living. I learned early in life that one cannot be fully in tune with God or fulfill His purpose for their life if they're constantly worried about money. I will not discuss high-level finance, how to invest in the stock market, per se, or how to become the next millionaire. There are plenty of books on the market for those topics. There's no point in aiming to be a millionaire if you haven't yet learned to manage the money you have. It doesn't matter how much money you make, if your behavior and thought process are to be a spender and not a saver, planner, or giver, managing your finances is going to be challenging. *"Well done, good and faithful servant. You have been faithful over a little; I will set you over much. Enter into the joy of your master."*[c] If you are faithful (at managing) a few things, God will put you in charge of many things. Why should God bless you with more of anything when you have not well-managed what he has already given you? Applying wisdom to your financial decisions will produce better outcomes.

I use biblical principles and illustrations throughout the book because God's principles for managing money are universal and provide the best guidance for any financial situation. He must have anticipated the struggles because there are over 2,000 Bible references to money and possessions--twice the number of references to prayer and faith combined. Given the emphasis on money, one can only surmise that our spiritual life is connected to our relationship with money. The amount of debt and the increasing number of public storage facilities tell the story of greed and excess. But it doesn't have to be your story. This book will give you an opportunity to write your financial success story.

You need wisdom to help you manage your finances. The easiest way to get wisdom is to simply ask for it. *"If any one of you lacks wisdom, let him ask God, who gives generously to all without reproach, and it will be given him."*[d] If you don't know something or how to apply your knowledge, ask God for direction. He will freely give you the wisdom you need to make good choices. Don't expect a large thunderous voice to speak from the clouds.

Wisdom can be obtained by:

- ***Consulting God's word.*** The Bible is filled with wise counsel, particularly the books of Proverbs and Ecclesiastes.

- ***Engaging individuals experienced in life.*** Talking with others who have experienced the challenges you're facing will be very beneficial.

- ***Seeking professional resources***. Speak with professionals experienced in a specific area like a personal finance coach or other experts in the financial arena. Read personal finance books based on Godly principles.

- ***Living***. The most critical way to gain wisdom is to observe others and learn from their mistakes, as well as your own. There is no better teacher than one's life experiences--the good, bad, and the ugly.

Engaging older or more experienced people appears to be a challenge for some millennials. Because you are extremely knowledgeable, there's a sense of over confidence that is carelessly applied to life situations and often yields bad results simply because you lacked wisdom in making decisions. You'd rather rely on information found on the Internet or the opinion and advice of your peers, who have no more life experience, rather than seek the wisdom of someone who has already been down the path you're headed. That's not to say that you shouldn't consult your friends on various issues. However, people in your circle typically share the same thoughts and values, and they have limited experiences. If you want to get a broader perspective on a situation or decision, you must enlarge your territory of resources.

Perhaps you're hesitant to ask for guidance from older acquaintances, parents, or bosses because you feel you'll be unfairly judged or thought of as less competent. The reality is that these individuals would love nothing more than for you to seek their advice. *"Listen to advice and accept instruction, that you may gain wisdom in the future."*[e] There's nothing to be lost in seeking guidance or another perspective before making important financial decisions.

As you continue reading, make a note of opportunities where you can apply wisdom to your financial decisions. Applying wisdom on your journey to better managing your money will yield positive, long lasting results for living a debt free and more fruitful life. I hope you're excited as I am to be taking this journey together.

CHAPTER 1

It's Not (all) Your Fault and You Are Not Alone

No temptation has overtaken you that is not common to man. (1 Corinthians 10:13a)

I f you are between the ages of 18 and 34, you are officially a member of the largest generation in the United States,[1] affectionately known as "millennials." Your generation does not like to be "boxed in" or labeled, and the term "millennial" may not appeal all that much to you; particularly since it's typically connected to everything that's wrong with America. Don't believe the bad hype. If there is a measure of truth in the stereotypes attributed to your generation, rest assured you did not wake up like that. Generations before you helped to shape or influence the person you've become as it relates to your attitude about life and more specifically about money. Let's take a short stroll back in time.

Generationalists study the behavior and attitude of different generations and how historical or major social events influence social norms of groups of people who are coming of age during these events Each generation is assigned a nickname based on certain themes of those times. Individuals affected by those events tend to share similar attitudes and behaviors towards lifestyle choices, such as careers, family (whether they want marriage and children), where they want to live, politics, and money.

Money is one of the more prevalent areas that differentiate generations. Each generation; Generation Xers (Gen Xers), baby boomers, and traditionalists think and behave differently when it comes to dealing with money or finances. The differences in attitudes explain why your parents and grandparents often disagree with some of your financial decisions.

I attended a seminar at an accounting trade conference last year. One of the presenters, Meghan Johnson, co-author of *Generations, Inc.* and a Gen Xer, told the story of how she planned an evening out with her grandmother. Running short of time, Meghan called ahead to make sure her grandmother would be ready to leave right away. When Meghan arrived at her grandmother's home, she found Grandma enjoying an evening martini. Because they were running late, Meghan suggested that her grandmother pour the drink in the sink. She told Grandma she would order another drink at the restaurant. Her grandmother refused to dump the drink and thought it was ridiculous that Meghan would suggest such a wasteful thing.

Meghan's grandmother is a traditionalist. Born between 1926 and 1945, Grandma was a young adult during the Great Depression, a time when the country was in its worst economic downturn. The stock market crash of 1929 was the beginning of the Great Depression. Your generation's, economic equivalent is the recession of 2008. During the Great Depression, many people lost their life savings, and a substantial number of them committed suicide. Traditionalists lived through two wars. Jobs were scarce, and money was even less, so they held onto both very tightly. There was no such thing as job hopping. The economic conditions created a waste-not-want-not attitude, which explains Grandma's reaction to Meghan's foolish suggestion to throw away a perfectly good drink.

Compare the traditionalists with the generation that followed called the baby boomers who were born between 1946 and 1964. They're called baby boomers because when men were returning from war, women were coming out of the factories, and the mood throughout the country was very optimistic. There was a lot of reconnecting that resulted in the explosion of babies born each year during this period.

Baby boomers came of age during the 1970s and 1980s when young adults were passionately protesting many social causes like the Civil Rights movement and the Vietnam War. They were carefree and uninhibited in their indulgence in sex, drugs, and Rock and Roll music. Financially, because this generation had great jobs and worked hard (typically staying with one company their entire careers), boomers had more discretionary income than any other generation, which allowed them to spend on luxuries. Credit was easily available bringing with it high levels of debt. Baby boomers view their success in relation to their job titles, salaries, and their toys. They live the American dream, which is symbolized by having great jobs, big homes, two cars, 2.5 children, and a dog. Their general attitude about money is that they are entitled to their excessive lifestyle because they work hard.

Boomers are America's sweethearts who largely represent America's backbone--the middle class. These prosperous post-war individuals had the privilege of going to college for little or no costs because of government grants. Through education and innovation, they positioned themselves to meet their financial goals. Even those who did not go to college enjoyed high paying jobs in industries such as steel and automobile manufacturing. Boomers took full advantage of opportunities that came with a thriving economy.

However, boomers' lack of oversight in preparing or sustaining a healthy economy for future generations is undeniable. Since the Bush (W) administration, boomer policymakers adopted policies that allowed college costs to double. They failed to invest enough in new training programs for young workers who, at one time, could depend on factory jobs. They passed trade policies that allowed millions of jobs to go overseas and allowed the national debt to increase at an alarming rate.[2] These events would eventually lead to the demise of programs designed to provide financial assistance to young people entering college. The policies resulted in astronomical student loan debt being forced on the next generation.

One downfall of the boomers is that they aren't too good at saving money for their retirement. Many of them find themselves financially unprepared for this life event. Senior citizens are continuing to work when they should be relaxing and reaping the benefits of their working years. It saddens me when I go to Walmart or McDonald's and see senior citizens who must work to supplement their social security income. Chapter Nine talks about the importance of millennials preparing for this life event as soon as possible.

Next in line are Gen Xers who were born between 1965 and 1988. This generation grew up watching their parents, the baby boomers, chase the American dream. Often, their parents' desire for more "stuff" meant missing out on recitals and football games. Independence was learned at an early age. Gen Xers were Latchkey kids; they came home from school to spend hours alone before their parents arrived from work. This lack of parental oversight made Gen Xers resolve to do things differently. They wanted more work-life balance in their careers and required their work to be fulfilling. Gen Xers are the helicopter parents who hover over you while guiding your every move and helping you avoid negative consequences. They spend money to buy more house, more car, and more clothes than they need or can afford. They also carry the most debt of any other generation and were most impacted by the 2008 recession. During the recession, many Gen Xers lost the value of their homes and investments, and many of them lost their jobs.

And finally, there's your unique generation. It sounds like you could be the star of your own movie. Imagine the voiceover by the baritone-voiced guy who does the movie trailers, "Coming in September...THE MILLENNIALS." I find it amusing that the generation who detests labels has the coolest label of them all. I digress.

Seriously, you are a member of a very special sector of the population with unique attributes and challenges. There's no doubt that millennials are the most analyzed generation. Being the largest generation in America, people are paying attention to you. Marketers want to know how to capture your attention to convince you that you need their products. Banks are changing the way they present their financial services and providing mobile options. Restaurants are changing their menus to accommodate millennial eating habits and preferences. You should be aware of marketing tactics that attempt to persuade you that you need their products and services when you really don't.

Part of what makes you unique is that you have come of age at a time when technology is growing at the fastest rate ever. You are the techie generation who can multi-task by juggling multiple devices at the same time. Your smartphone is your lifeline and allows you to fit your phone, computer, alarm clock, camera, GPS, and entertainment in the palm of your hand. You are the go-to people for previous generations when it comes to technology. I always smile when I think of my 78-year-old dad who loves to work on old cars and has never even touched a computer. One day he was commenting on not being able to find a part he needed for an old car he was fixing up. I supposed he'd been driving all over town looking for this part. While at dinner, the conversation morphed into talking about the difficulty of locating the part. Suddenly, he turned to my daughter and asked, "Can't you just Google it?"

As a member of the smartest generation, you have a flair for creativity and entrepreneurship, and you willingly and eagerly embrace change and learning new things. You are expressive and opinionated. You use technology in the most innovative ways so that you work smarter not harder. Can I let you in on a little secret? Although Gen Xers and boomers may give you a tough time, they really do admire you. Many of them would say that you frustrate them to no end. But deep inside, they love your zest for life, your love for adventure, and your do-what-makes-you-happy mantra. I think they may even be a little jealous—but that's our little secret.

It's puzzling how a group of people with so many positive attributes can also be known as spoiled, lazy, narcissistic, selfie-loving, and entitled. The word on the street is that you want everything your parents have, and you want it today. "They" say that you think you deserve shorter working hours, four weeks of vacation, and promotion within six months of being hired. If any of this is true for you, I'm happy to tell you that your attitude may not be your fault completely.

Those who perpetuate millennial stereotypes don't often understand some of the factors that have contributed to the economic challenges you face today. Boomers and Gen Xers' behavior influences the millennial mindset when it comes to money. Essentially, you are the monsters the boomers created! Most children mimic the behavior of their parents. If the family take vacations, buy cars, and purchase furniture and clothing using debt, this becomes the acceptable way of doing things. Why wait when you can have it now?

Gen Xers work long hours, and if they were raised in a two-parent household, chances are both parents worked because the status symbols had become the luxury car and oversized house, and the debt must be paid. Spending extensive amounts of time away from the kids often brought feelings of guilt, and so guilt-parenting was born. Gen Xers withheld discipline and indulged you in material things to make up for their absences. They made sure you had the best of everything and eagerly supported designer brands. You reflect Gen Xers' parenting skills and their ability to provide. Your parents demanded that you were issued a trophy for every extra-curricular activity in which you participated—even if your team lost. How dare society calls you entitled! Wearing expensive clothing, participating in multiple activities, and having the most expensive birthday celebrations showcased the best of your parents and what they wanted others to see. You were shown the pleasures of materialism and taught that waiting was not an option. If you want it now, charge it. Unfortunately, Gen Xers aren't living the America dream; they're borrowing it.

The Great Recession of 2008 was the beginning of a period when the economy took a spiraling fall. The main cause was due to banks loaning money to individuals who could not afford to repay their loans, which left a shortage of funds for the banks. Without the banks being able to loan money, spending slowed, and housing prices fell leaving homeowners with negative wealth. People lost jobs, particularly those who worked in the mortgage, homebuilding and real estate industries, and consumer confidence bottomed out.

This is the economy you inherited as you prepared to enter the workforce, eager and bright-eyed, only to find there were no jobs. The available jobs did not pay very well. Many of you settled for jobs totally unrelated to your college studies just so that you would have some measure of income. The recession forced you to delay adulthood by continuing to be financially dependent on your parents, and many of you reluctantly moved back home.

You've been dealt a bad hand, and your struggle is real. However, some of you have not played your hands so well. I've witnessed many of you struggling to navigate your finances. You haven't always figured out the best way to spend that paycheck, and you must make tough decisions. Do you let the student loan payment slip this month and pay the rent instead? Or do you make the student loan payment and be late on the rent? Do you change jobs to make more money? Or do you hang on to your job and hope for a promotional opportunity?

Sometimes your priorities get mixed up, and you find yourselves forced with dire consequences. Lacking wisdom, millennials make bad financial decisions, like buying concert tickets not knowing where you'll get the remainder of your rent money, maxing out your credit cards on an item you *must have* because it's on sale, or taking the vacation you can't afford. Even though you inherited a crappy economy, you owe it to yourself to respond in a responsible, mature manner. You must make wiser decisions by delaying gratification, practicing self-discipline, and distancing yourself from negative influences, all of which will derail your plans of becoming financially healthy. If you're struggling financially because of lack of knowledge and wisdom and are recovering from bad decisions, you are not alone.

My life journey includes serving in my church as a Sunday School teacher and facilitator of small group studies whose participants are millennials. I also work as an Accounting Manager for a local government agency in which forty percent of my team are millennials. It's been my joy getting to know some of these millennials on a personal level. My team members, students, and my two millennial children are the inspiration for this book. They've provided me numerous opportunities to dispense wisdom and practical advice on personal finances. I've discovered that their financial struggles are no different than what many other millennials are facing. As you read some of their profiles below, you may find that pieces of their stories resemble some of your challenges. Let's start with Chloe.

Chloe is a 28-year old accounting assistant who frequently expresses her frustrations of living on a $38,000 salary. She's single with no children and lives in a studio apartment because it's the only living space she can afford. One of her goals is to run a non-profit agency that focuses on teaching life skills to young girls. She also wants to have a family. Other goals include sending her future kids to college, living comfortably, and being able to take nice vacations.

Chloe owns a 13-year-old car that was passed down from her parents and has no car payment. Her current debt includes a

$20,000 student loan balance that had been in default. Her parents helped pull her out of default by making the required triple payments. Months later, Chloe started missing payments again. Chloe constantly receives traffic violations that go unpaid. She even earned a court appearance to address the violations. She regularly receives final notices of past due cell phone and car insurance bills.

Chloe's favorite and frequent activities include attending music festivals—in and out of town, hanging out with friends for happy hour, eating out with her boyfriend, and frequenting thrift stores. The good news is that Chloe has a savings account. The sad news is the account has a balance of only $400.

David is 25-years old and has been in the military for about seven years. He joined the military shortly after graduating high school. When he left home, he took his second-hand car that his parents purchased with cash. The car was only five years old when it was purchased and in terrific shape when David left. Less than a month after arriving at his first duty assignment, David traded the car in for a more stylish used car. Apparently, the car no longer matched his "image." For the first time, David had a car payment. A year later, while still carrying a loan balance for his second vehicle, he decided to upgrade his image again. The following year, the same thing. David is now paying on his fourth vehicle over a span of seven years. With each new trade, the loan balances were rolled into the financing for the newer vehicle, which made his monthly payment increase. Because of the loan balance rollovers, David is currently paying $1,000 per month, including car insurance, to drive from point A to point B.

David also likes to have the latest model cell phone and upgrades his phone with each new release. Clothing and shoes are important to David, and he buys clothing on a whim. And of course, the perfect outfit must have the perfect shoes to match. David estimates he spends $400 or more each month on clothing. He also eats out at least three times a week spending about $300 monthly. In addition to his monthly car expense, David has a credit card balance of $7,000 and pays the minimum amount due. He has a checking account that he consistently depletes to zero days before payday. He has no money in his savings account except the required $5 to keep the account active. David has expressed a desire to complete his college degree so that he's more marketable at the end of his military obligations, but he does not take advantage of the free education provided to military personnel. He spends his non-duty time playing intramural football, basketball, and video games.

Lastly, there's Lauren, 30, and Chase, 32. Lauren and Chase are married with two young children ages four and two. Lauren graduated from college with a degree in Psychology. However, she was not able to find a job in her field of study and has been working for an insurance company as a customer service supervisor making an annual salary of $36,000. She also has a student loan balance of $30,000 that is in deferment while she takes online courses toward a graduate degree in business administration. Lauren drives a four-year-old BMW that she purchased two years ago. The loan balance on the vehicle is $18,000 with monthly payments of $475.

Chase is a business analyst making $55,000 a year. The balance on his two-year-old Toyota 4-Runner that he purchased new is $22,000 with monthly payments of $500. Chase has no student loans. The couple has combined credit card debt of $15,000 from purchasing clothing, vacations, and furniture. They pay a little more than the minimum on the credit card bills. Their joint savings account balance is less than $1,000.

The family has been renting a two-bedroom apartment for the past five years. They realize the apartment is now too small for their family and want to purchase a home. Between the student loan debt, daycare, car loans, and credit card payments, they're finding it a challenge to come up with a monthly mortgage payment they can afford. If they can save a sizeable down payment, they can lower their monthly mortgage payments. Chase's mom, who is widowed, offered to allow the family to live with her for one year to save for their down payment. Chase and Lauren decided they would save $20,000 over the next year. Several months after moving in with Mom, things started to turn sour. Mom became frustrated as she witnessed Lauren and Chase's unbridled spending habits. After six months, they'd saved only $5,000 towards their goal.

These three profiles capture behavior that is prominent throughout the lives of some millennials. It's very clear that many of you are having financial challenges that include not being able to save money. In a survey by the American Institute of Certified Public Accountants,[2] when asked what is preventing millennials from saving, the responses were as follows:

- 84% said that your current salary was not sufficient

- 81% said you simply had too many bills

- 79% responded that you were working on paying down debt

- 62 % said that not having a budget makes savings difficult

- 44% of you do not pay your credit cards in full each month

- 41% of you have less than $100 in your checking account

- 30% of you have paid late or overdraft fees

- 23% of you have missed paying a bill

These statistics reveal some reasons why many of you are living paycheck to paycheck. Whether the behavior is from lack of knowledge, wisdom, or both, clearly intervention is necessary to assist you in getting to a better financial place. I believe most of you would manage your money better if you knew how and understood the ramifications of not doing so.

Consider this: Only 24% of millennials demonstrate basic financial knowledge. Over 50% of millennials said they don't feel "savvy" when it comes to investing. Over half of the older millennials said they didn't receive enough training on managing finances while in school."[1] That's not surprising given that only 17 states require high school students to take a course in personal finance.[2] The purpose of high school is to educate and prepare students to function as productive citizens. Given the enormity of negative consequences when finances are not properly managed, personal finance should be a requirement for the successful completion of high school.

Following the principles and advice in this book will make a dramatic difference in your life and that of your loved ones for whom you are financially responsible. Change is not always easy. I promise that if you have a sincere desire to change your situation, that's half the battle. Desire, effort, and some stick-to-it-ness are all you need to be successful.

You're probably thinking, "Oh no, here we go. She's going to tell me how I can enjoy life 30 years from now if I sacrifice all my fun and save all my money!" Relax. You won't have to wait 30 years to start enjoying life. By rethinking "fun" and gaining new priorities, you can enjoy an abundant life right now. However, your ability to enjoy life 30 years from now depends on what you do today. Since we know millennials are known for their willingness to embrace change and try new things, I believe you are up for the challenge.

If you want to be financially healthy, you're going to have to embrace a new way of thinking and learn new behaviors that align with your goals. *"Do not be conformed to this world, but be transformed by the renewal of your mind, that by testing you may discern what is the will of God, what is good and acceptable and perfect."*[a] You'll come to understand that you cannot do things the same way as everyone else. Spending mindlessly, living above your means, and acquiring unnecessary debt is not what God wants for you. To move ahead to a better financial picture, you must refrain from what has become "acceptable." Embracing new things begins with letting go of stinking thinking. This kind of thinking is embracing the mentality that you must be in line with the rest of the world. Stinking thinking says it's normal to be in debt, to buy the oversized house, expensive car, or clothing you can't afford. It's stinking thinking that says everything you do is for yourself, and giving to others like the church or charity is old school. Embracing change is about understanding that you are here for a greater purpose.

In every area of your life, particularly finances, you should be a shining example of God's goodness. Managing your money in ways that honor and glorify God makes you the beacon the world can look to. He wants to show you off. God wants to show His best work through your lives. Your job is to put yourself in a position so He can build up His showcase. Once you understand the importance of properly managing your money and the impact of failing to do so, you'll gain a new perspective that will propel you to behave differently.

In managing my group of millennial accounting clerks, I have trainers who conduct one-on-one training for new accounting clerks. Kaley was assigned to train our newest hire, Jason. Her training method consisted of giving Jason a copy of the written procedures for entering invoices into the financial system. Kaley told Jason that he could come to see her if he had any questions. It seemed that Jason caught on rather quickly and was soon processing a considerable number of invoices. After a few weeks, he became bored and started making multiple errors.

After learning that Jason was having performance issues, I decided he needed additional training. I assigned him to Alicia who approached training differently. Alicia began her training by explaining to Jason the importance of his job. She told him that he's responsible for ensuring citizens' tax money is spent wisely. Therefore, his audit of the invoices before entering them into the financial system was critical. Alicia explained that errors could result in duplicate payments that could impact department budgets or lose taxpayers' money if the overpayments aren't recouped. A few weeks later, Jason's error rate had decreased significantly. The process for entering invoices had not changed. What made the difference? Once Jason understood the importance and purpose of his job, he approached it with renewed interest. His attitude changed, and because his attitude changed, his behavior changed.

You are no different than Jason. When you understand why it's not a good idea to spend more than you make, why it's a good idea to delay that major purchase, or why you struggle to pay for necessities, you will begin to think differently. Once you understand the importance and reason for having a plan, you will have a different attitude and outlook about your finances and begin to spend more purposefully with your goals at the forefront of your mind. By thinking differently, you will behave differently. Bills are paid on time, frivolous spending ceases, debt is paid off, and you can save for big ticket items. Your bank account will thank you, your family will thank you, and more importantly, God will be pleased.

Even with all the challenges you face, and there are many, it is important for you to know that God wants you to live a life of joy and peace--the kind of peace that comes when you know everything is under control. When your finances are trashed, it's difficult to be at your best. You shouldn't be stressed out because of debt collectors. And as my mother used to say, you certainly shouldn't be "robbing Peter to pay Paul." God has a real purpose and plans for your life that do not include being enslaved by debt and money struggles. Do the wise thing by taking control of your money and managing it in a manner that makes sense. Let's continue this journey of discovering how to prepare yourself to live a financially healthy and debt free life.

* * *

1. Which of the three millennial profiles resonates with you the most, Chloe, David, or Lauren and Chase?

_____

_____

_____

_____

_____

2. Before now, what resources have you used to learn about managing your money?

_____

_____

_____

_____

_____

CHAPTER 2

Breaking Through the Barriers

*And he said to them, "Take care, and be on your guard
against all covetousness, for one's life does not consist in
the abundance of his possessions.* (Luke 12:15)

Although things are much better than they were eight years
ago, the economic fallout of 2008 continues to impact
many of your lives negatively. The thing about negative
situations is that you can choose your response to them. You can
complain and blame, but neither of those choices will make a
difference. Only what you *do* matters. You have legitimate reasons to
be discontented with the economy. But when you remove personal
responsibility, those reasons become excuses. And nobody likes
excuses. Excuses almost always bring negative consequences. "An
excuse is the most expensive brand of self-defeat you will ever
purchase."[1]

Where does personal responsibility start? What can you do to
make your financial situation better? What are you willing to
temporarily sacrifice to reach your financial goals?

If you're reading this book, my hope is that you've decided to
turn things around. Before starting out on any journey, you should
be aware of the roadblocks or barriers you might encounter. Your
journey to financial health is no different. There are three barriers

that threaten your ability to reach your financial goals. The barriers are a lack of self-control, procrastination, and comparative influences.

SELF-CONTROL

Of any other character trait, the ability to control yourself is one of the most important. To have self-control is to be able to control acting upon feelings, impulses, and desires for physical and material comfort that may have negative consequences. It's the ability to say "no" when you want to say "yes." It is doing what is necessary, even when it's difficult, knowing that refraining will yield better results. Galatians 5:23 lists self-control as one of the fruits of the Spirit or character trait essential to being successful, not only as a Christian but in everything you do. It is critical that you learn to exercise self-control as part of your continued efforts to curtail your spending.

When my son was in kindergarten, his report card had a grading category labeled, "Self-Control." His teacher, Mrs. Smith, was disappointed that my son was frequently challenged in this area. She and I discussed ways to help him become less impulsive. He had to learn that talking out of turn, getting out of his seat without permission, and distracting other students were not acceptable behaviors. I find it interesting that psychologists and educators consider self-control such an important life skill that the benchmark is included in the kindergarten curriculum. It makes sense that the earlier one learns to master self-control, the better off they'll be in every area of their life.

When my son failed to exercise self-control, he experienced negative consequences like forfeiting recess. In the same manner, when it comes to managing your money, a lack of self-control will bring negative consequences. Engaging in excessive impulsive spending may cause you to forfeit home ownership, a college education for you or your child, or the ability to enjoy your senior years. Sadly, the consequences may also include the demise of your relationships.

The need for instant gratification or the inability to delay gratification is the result of a lack of self-control. Gratification is a feeling of satisfaction or pleasure. Our brains are wired for gratification. There is an area in your brain called the nucleus accumbens that influences your feelings of pleasure. It also influences your tendency towards addictions. Gratification can come from food, experiences, sex, compliments, or shopping. In other words, if it makes you feel good, you want it. That's not necessarily a terrible thing. God gave you the sense of pleasure, and anything God provides is good. However, when your need for gratification is displaced, it causes problems. For example, you may have your eye on a new car but can't afford the payments until next year. You visit the dealership to just "browse" and the salesman convinces you to test drive the car of your dreams. Long story short, you buy the car and end up struggling to make the payments. *"The plans of the diligent lead surely to abundance, but everyone who is hasty comes only to poverty."*[a] When you continue to spend impulsively with no plan or goals, you'll soon realize that you won't have enough to meet your needs or wants.

Unfortunately, millennials have a reputation when it comes to instant gratification. Who can hardly blame you? Think about it; you're coming of age when everything is instant. You are the tech babies who are used to getting instant results like on-demand TV and instant messaging. When texting someone, if the response is not immediate, you feel anxious. When downloading a movie that takes too long, you consider a computer upgrade or purchasing a faster network. If you're making an online purchase, you pay the extra shipping charge to get it overnight. And, when the new iPhone is released you pitch a tent in front of the store 48 hours in advance and wait *"patiently."* There's nothing like being the first to have the latest and greatest thing along with bragging rights.

According to an article written by John Fleming for *Business Journal* and a recent Gallop poll, compared to other generations, millennials are most likely to shop for fun, make a purchase on impulse, and make a major purchase that costs at least one week's pay.[2] Impulse purchases and big-ticket purchases have increased significantly. There's no doubt that routinely buying on impulse hits your wallet very hard and is a major barrier to your ability to reach your goals. Ironically, 34% of you say that saving is your number one goal. Other goals include living healthy, paying off debt, and losing weight; however, 65% of you confess that your lack of saving is due to impulse spending.[3]

The bottom line is that many of you lack self-control when it comes to spending. Creating debt and realigning bills for impulse purchases is not okay and doesn't get you where you want to be. For a generation that wants things as quickly as possible, this should include your dreams and aspirations. The path to most dreams involves money. Take a moment and think about what you want out of life that will require money. Seriously. Pause right now and capture the vision in your mind of all the things you want to accomplish or acquire [PAUSE]. Each time you spend money on impulsive items you delay making your vision a reality.

Practicing delayed gratification is how you overcome the pattern of destructive spending. When you exercise self-control by not giving in to the urge to splurge, you are learning to delay gratification--the ability to wait to buy those things you want until you can afford them. It will take time to train yourself to this new way of behaving, and it won't be easy. You'll be tested at every turn. You have help in Jesus. In John 1:4-5, Jesus talks about the vine and the branches. To produce good fruit (self-control), you (the branch) must connect to the vine. Jesus is that vine. Through the work of His Spirit, you have the power within you to resist the urge to splurge. Praying before making purchases will lead you to make the right decisions. Without the power of the Holy Spirit, you are going to continually struggle with self-control in every area of your life, including finances.

Listed below are some practical ways to exercise self-control and avoid the consequences of impulse buying:

Give yourself some time. Don't be in such a hurry to commit to buying an item you've selected. Whether it's in a store or shopping online, wait 30 minutes before buying. That's the recommended time to decide if you really need something. When I do this, 90% of the time I don't purchase. Amazon makes it easy for you to complete your online purchases by not giving you time to think about it. They came up with the clever idea of the one-click purchase. Amazon realizes that if you spend time going through the multi-step ordering process, you may change your mind.

Don't shop when you are emotional or hungry. Retail therapy is real. Shopping temporarily lifts your mood and provides instant gratification. If you're emotional or upset about something, go for a walk or participate in some other physical activity. Exercise is an instant mood booster, and the results are much more appealing. Do not—I repeat—do not go into a grocery store when you're hungry. Your stomach and your mind team up to convince you that everything looks delicious, and you leave with much more than you planned.

Plan your purchases. When you need to go shopping, whether at the mall or the grocery store, make sure you take a list of the things you need. Stick to your list. If you go to the mall with the purpose of buying a white shirt, buy the white shirt and leave. You'll feel good about sticking with your plan once you get home. If you continue to browse, you're going to purchase something that you don't need.

Avoid shopping with shop-a-holics. We all have at least one friend (or perhaps it's you) who is the consummate shopper. Do not shop with these people. They will convince you to buy things you do not need. You may feel compelled to purchase things simply to be an active participant.

Don't get suckered by the clearance or "one-day-only" sales. Most major department stores have one-day-only sales several times a year. Their marketing leads you to believe that you'll miss out on some great deal if you don't come to this sales event. This is an area that challenges many of you. Millennials are known to be bargain shoppers. You buy items that you can't pass up because they're on clearance—with an additional 40% off. Think back to that Black Friday deal on the big screen TV that was almost a giveaway. It didn't have all the features you wanted, but for the price, you couldn't pass it up. Unfortunately, after three months you realized it didn't quite fit the bill, and you ended up purchasing the one you really wanted and selling the bargain TV on eBay. Getting a great deal is only a smart move if you need it and can afford it.

Question yourself. When contemplating a purchase, ask yourself four questions:

- How is this purchase going to improve my life?
- Will purchasing this item get me closer to my goals?
- How much use will I get out of this item?
- Does my budget allow for the purchase?

Be honest with yourself and don't attempt to rationalize or over sell the item to yourself. I have a tool I use to help me reconsider a purchase. I cut a neon-colored piece of paper into the size of a dollar bill. The four questions are written on this paper and placed with my dollar bills and debit card in my wallet. When I access my wallet to pay for an item, I see the neon paper that reminds me to pause and reconsider. On many occasions, I've asked the cashier to return an item. The first few times I felt a little embarrassed. Eventually, it didn't matter to me what the sales clerk thought. I'd go home feeling proud of myself for having exercised self-control. If it helps, feel free to create a visual reminder that works for you.

These suggestions will get you started on your path to practicing self-control. You'll be able to see the money saved from not giving in. Use the money to pay down debt or add to your savings, which will advance you towards your financial goals.

PROCRASTINATION

The second barrier that keeps you from meeting your goals, financial or otherwise, is procrastination. Everyone procrastinates to a degree. "I'll get to it tomorrow," is what you tell yourself. Yet, days, weeks, months, and years pass, and you still haven't taken one step towards completing a task or project. Simply put, procrastination is the unnecessary putting off or avoidance of an action you need to take. You delay or fail to complete tasks even when you know there will be negative consequences. Things happen, and I get that. We've all chosen to do other things to avoid a dreaded task. Something more appealing catches your time and attention. But, when you intentionally and habitually redirect your efforts to other activities to avoid doing something that you know you should be doing, you are participating in destructive behavior. Procrastination of this nature yields missed opportunities and almost always costs you money. Not to mention that it causes stress and robs you of your joy and peace. Procrastination is a dream snatcher and a major roadblock to financial freedom.

As millennials, you're likely to have been labeled lazy because of your tendency to procrastinate. Author Isrealmore Ayivor describes laziness this way; "Laziness is when your sleep overcomes your passion, not under the influence of drugs, but under the control of excuses and procrastination."[4] This may be true for some of you. What critics fail to understand is that in your technology driven culture, you are accustomed to seeking information and getting results in a flash. I'm sure you can recall being engaged in discussion with your peers when a question of fact comes up. What's the first thing you do? You Google it on your smartphone. Immediately, with very little effort, you have the answer in the palm of your hands.

In addition to technology's capability for lightening-speed research, as you grew into adulthood, many of you had the consistent help of "helicopter" parents who hovered over you ready to take care of any situation that caused you the slightest bit of distress. While Gen Xers learned to figure things out on their own, most millennials had only to show frustration and wave the white flag of surrender, and a parent swooped in for the rescue. I once had a coworker who would come to work completely exhausted because he pulled all-nighters working on his son's *college* papers while his son lay in bed resting for the next day's classes. What?

My daughter, Danielle, is a high school English teacher and occasionally shares her classroom experiences with me. One story involved a student who received a failing grade on a writing assignment. He was given the opportunity to resubmit the paper to improve his grade. When he resubmitted the paper, it was perfect and filled with a higher level of vocabulary and other inconsistencies. It was obvious the student had not written the paper. When Danielle approached the student with her concerns, he admitted that his dad "helped" with the paper. She decided to contact the parent. After first giving my daughter a few choice words and threatening to contact the school administrator, Dad finally calmed himself and defeatedly admitted that he probably went too far in helping his son. As the conversation progressed, the exasperated dad posed a question. "Can you please tell me how far is too far when you are trying to help your child?"

You may be asking how this relates to procrastination. My theory is that when a person has little or no experience handling the more challenging aspects of life, their ability or willingness to be proactive in getting things done is hindered. It's as if they go through a mental wait-and-see mode wishing that somehow the task is going to get done on its own, that someone will come in and rescue them, or perhaps the situation will go away altogether. As a millennial who wants quick and easy results, many of you find it challenging to maneuver situations and tasks that require a significant amount of time and effort. Things that stress you out just thinking about them cause you to divert your attention elsewhere. As a result, important tasks are delayed or not completed.

One reason procrastination is prevalent in your lives is that many of you seem to lack a proper perspective of time. God created you to fulfill a certain purpose on this earth. You were also given a certain amount of time to walk in your purpose. Most of you don't spend a whole lot of time dwelling on the fact that you are not going to live forever. According to the Center for Disease Control, you get an average of about 79 years to exercise this gift called life.[5] That may seem like a lot of time but trust me, it's not. The average age of the millennial demographic is 26. At 26 years of age, you have already spent 33% of your gift. That's 1/3rd of your life gone, never to be seen again. I don't want to sound morbid or project doom and gloom, but these are the cold hard facts. The question I ask of you is this: How do you want to spend the remaining 67% of your life?

If you want to get the most out of your life and live a life of blessings, service, and abundance, it is important that you learn to manage your money. I honestly believe no one wants to spend any portion of their 67% climbing out of debt or struggling to make ends meet. God has so much more planned for your life. *"For I know the plans I have for you, declared the Lord, plans for welfare and not for evil, to give you a future and a hope."*[b] Those plans include living free from debt and financial worries so you can live out your life and your purpose stress-free. It's a life of outward and inward blessings that bring glory and honor to God. It's a life where your material blessings are not a mere display of your wealth or prestige but a witness of God's favor over your life.

Time is one of the most precious gifts God has given you. When someone gives you a gift, the expectation is that you show appreciation by treating it with care. Your life is no different. One way to express your gratitude is by making the best use of your time. *"Teach us to number our days that we may get a heart of wisdom."*[c] When you realize how short life is, you won't squander your time by frequently procrastinating; instead, you will wisely and purposefully redeem your time.

Don't waste time wasting time. *"Whatever your hand finds to do, do it with your might."*[d] When it comes to getting your finances under control, don't waste time contemplating whether you're going to create a budget or monitor your spending. Whatever you need to do to reach your goals, don't put it off. The sooner you get started, the more quality time you'll have to live the life God intended for you.

I've listed five other reasons below why millennials procrastinate.[6] As you read through them, take an honest look at what may be *your* reason(s). If any of them resonate with you, acknowledge it and commit to making a change.

Being a perfectionist. Perfectionists focus too much on being perfect. Since no one is perfect, it seems to follow that imperfect people can't produce perfect results. That's not to say that you shouldn't put your best foot forward. However, needing flawless outcomes is a problem when you spend an inordinate amount of time thinking about the task and planning to do it but never taking any action. King Solomon warned about waiting for the perfect time to accomplish a task. *"He who observes the wind will not sow, and he who regards the clouds will not reap."*[e] Get your head out of the clouds and hit the ground running towards your goals. There is never going to be an absolutely perfect time to act. My mom used to tell me, "If you think long, you think wrong."

Fear of failure. You may never get around to starting or completing important tasks because you fear failure or rejection. No one succeeds in everything all the time, and those who have any measure of success have had their fair share of failures along the way. Failure is usually a prerequisite for success. Ask yourself, "What is the worst thing that can happen?" A famous dad shared words of wisdom with his daughters after they expressed disappointment that their team was defeated. He encouraged them by saying, "The only thing that's the end of the world is the end of the world." Whatever the outcome, if it's not the one you want, chalk it up to experience. If nothing else, you now know what to avoid on the next try. When learning how to manage a budget, you will not get it right on the first try. I'm telling you this now so that you don't fear starting the budget process. It may take you a few tries to semi-perfect it. There is only one situation where failure is inevitable, and that is the situation in which you fail to try.

If you fear you won't measure up, who do you measure yourself against? The only person you must compete with is yourself. There is always going to be someone who does "it" better, but they are not your standard. If you have a mission to accomplish, the only way to gauge your success is to measure it against your efforts. Your results will reflect your effort. If you give minimum effort, your results will be minimal. If you give your best effort, there's a greater chance that your results will prove successful.

I love to write. I've used what I consider to be one of my talents in service to my church by writing plays for the worship arts ministry. I also love working with young people and have done so as a mentor and teacher of Bible study for teens and young adults for over 20 years. Managing my finances and helping others navigate their financial challenges are other things I enjoy. When I began reflecting on my experiences and seeking my purpose, I didn't know that God would have me stir all three of my passions together for His benefit. The idea of writing a personal finance book for young adults began to take shape; however, I procrastinated for several years. I spoke about it often but did nothing. Do you know why? Fear. Despite my passion for the project, fear made me procrastinate. I feared not knowing how to start, that no one would be interested, that I wouldn't measure up to the Dave Ramseys and Ron Blues of the world—two highly regarded personal finance authors. But, I realized that unlike you, I don't have 67% of my life remaining. I only have 33%, and it's important for me to walk in my purpose of helping you gain control of your finances so that you can live out *your* purpose uninhibited by financial worries. The greater lesson that God taught me is to not worry about who has gone before me. My gift and purpose are uniquely crafted for me by God, and so is yours. Whether we reach one person or one million people, it's all by divine design.

Whatever your task, you must courageously get off your butt and forge ahead despite your fears. *"God has not given us a spirit of fear, but of power, and of love, and of a sound mind."*[f] God has given us the power to accomplish anything that's in His will despite any difficulties we face. Getting your finances in order may not be easy, but you can rest easy knowing that God's power is your source for success.

Lack of goals. If you haven't set any goals or are not actively working towards them, there's a 100% guarantee you won't meet them. Having no agenda or goals causes you to wander aimlessly through life reacting to situations as opposed to proactively working towards achieving your goals. Having no goals also causes you to spend money carelessly instead of intentionally. What do you want your financial future to resemble? What are you doing to make that picture a reality? Start with a realistic view of your current financial situation. Your immediate vision should align with your current means. For example, you can't realistically set a goal of owning a 3,500 sq. ft home on the hill next week or travel to all the continents if you're jobless and living with your parents. But you can envision having a job by next month. Notice that I didn't tell you that you *can't* have the 3,500 sq. ft home or that you *can't* travel. You just can't do those things next week. What you *can* do is start preparing and planning so that you can be in a financial position to have or do those things in the future. There is a process to achieving your financial goals.

When setting your goals, make sure they are SMART; they must be <u>S</u>pecific, <u>M</u>easurable, <u>A</u>chievable, <u>R</u>ealistic, and <u>T</u>imely. Write your goals down in priority order and reference them frequently. For example, your goals may look something like this:

- Pay down debt; pay 30% more than the minimum; finish by January 2019

- Increase giving this year by $1,000; contribute $83 more per month

- Save $10,000 for down payment on home; save $330 per month for 30 months

- Travel to Maui in a year; cost is $2,500, save $208 per month for 12 months

These goals are specific, the progress can be measured, they are achievable and realistic, and deadlines are assigned. Consider your income when setting timelines. Some financial experts would tell you never to consider buying a home or the trip to Maui until all your debt is paid in full, and that is great advice. However, because it's *your* budget, you get to set the priorities and determine how quickly you want to progress toward each of your goals. You can tackle them one at a time or simultaneously. If you address them simultaneously, you may need to either extend the deadlines or increase your income. The idea is to ***not add*** to your debt and not ***suspend*** or decrease your current debt payments to fund any of your other goals. The benefit of addressing them one at a time, with debt being eliminated first, is that you will free up money to apply to other goals. It also gives you the opportunity to practice delayed gratification. Your success in meeting your goals will be determined by the sacrifices you're willing to make.

You feel overwhelmed. Some millennials love to multitask and frequently take on multiple projects at once. Perhaps you have multiple projects or tasks because you've procrastinated, and now your tasks are piled high and appear insurmountable. So, what do you do with all the things you have on your plate? Nothing. You do nothing because you have no idea where to start. When you are overwhelmed it causes stress, and people naturally avoid stressful activities. Instead of handling one task at a time, you lose focus and involve yourself with mundane, no-stress activities like social media or Netflix.

If you're overwhelmed, it may be a matter of learning to prioritize your tasks and better manage your time. Start by identifying those tasks with deadlines. Create a to-do list and order tasks by their due dates. The severity of the consequences (if the task is not completed) should drive the priority. For each item on your to-do list, outline the steps necessary for completion. Focus on one item at a time and the related tasks. See my sample to-do list:

Merrie's To Do List 10/1/16 – 10/7/16

1. 10/2/16 - Complete Chapter 7 of book (~~research topic~~, ~~read resource articles~~, write)

2. 10/4/16 - Family budget meeting (get/bring quotes for new refrigerator)

3. 10/5/16 - Teach young adult bible study (~~read/study lesson~~, make outline, gather materials)

4. 10/7/16 - Prepare dancers for Christmas production (select song, choreograph, schedule rehearsal)

I've listed the various goals I need to meet. The tasks that must be completed to reach my goals are in parenthesis. As I complete my tasks, I line through them. For my fourth task, although the event doesn't happen for another two months, there are things I need to do to avoid last minute rushing. I allow myself a cushion so that if something comes up that causes me to delay completing a task, I can move the task to the following week and give it a higher priority.

Try to avoid repeatedly moving a task from one week to the next. This is still procrastination. The only difference is that you're documenting it. Breaking goals into manageable pieces and assigning realistic deadlines will keep you from feeling overwhelmed.

The format of the to-do list shown above is to give you an idea of how to track your progression in completing your tasks. As you might suspect, there's an app for that! Three popular apps that allow you to create to-do lists with due dates, sync your calendars, and share your lists with others are; *Any.do*, *Wunderlist*, and *Remember the Milk*. The apps are free and available for both Android and iOS. Don't be tempted to purchase the premium versions. The free versions offer enough features to help you stay on top of things.

Laziness. If none of the reasons above for procrastinating resonated with you, there's a good chance that your unwillingness to act is due to plain old laziness. That's a term to which no one wants their name associated. Merriam Webster's online dictionary defines lazy as, "not liking to work hard or be active; not having much activity; moving slowly." When you consider this definition, most people have experienced some moments of laziness. It becomes a problem when this "feeling" of not wanting to do anything is habitual. You tell yourself you'll get it done eventually, but right now you just don't care all that much. The Bible has many warnings for those who are lazy.

- *"Through sloth (laziness), the roof sinks in, and through indolence (inactivity) the house leaks."*[g]

- *"The sluggard (a lazy person) does not plow in the autumn; he will seek at harvest and have nothing."*[h]

- *"The soul of the sluggard craves and gets nothing, while the soul of the diligent is richly supplied."[i]*

If you've identified your reasons for procrastinating, that's a good start. Being aware makes it easier to avoid. Continual procrastination will ensure that wherever you're going, and whatever your goals, you certainly are not going to reach them as quickly as you could. Don't continue down the road of putting off tasks only to end up with regrets and a depleted bank account. Some of the consequences of procrastination include:

- Paying more than you should for travel expenses like flight or hotel reservations.

- Paying to treat serious health condition because you waited too long to visit the doctor.

- Paying late fees on credit cards, utilities, rent, and traffic violations.

- Strained work relationships. Missed promotional opportunities or termination due to habitually missing deadlines.

- Strained personal relationships. Family and friends can't trust you to get things done, which may result in feelings of resentment.

- Making poor decisions or haphazardly completing tasks due to rushing at the last minute.

Procrastination is not only costly in terms of lost financial opportunities. It may also cost you your reputation. *"A good name is to be chosen rather than great riches, and favor (respect) is better than silver or gold."* [j] Be a person of your word so that you earn the respect of others. A good reputation is far more precious than money.

COMPARATIVE INFLUENCES

The last of the three barriers to financial freedom is comparative influences. While writing this chapter, I attempted to come up with a term to describe influences in your life that cause you to compare yourself to others and develop feelings of inadequacy. I cleverly thought of the term "comparative influences." In my effort to avoid plagiarism, I did a Google search and wouldn't you know it? It already exists. There really is nothing new under the sun.

OxfordReference.com describes comparative influence as a type of influence exerted on consumers by their reference and peer groups. The group that has the most influence on you is the group that shares your beliefs, attitudes, and behaviors. You compare yourself to your peers (friends, contacts) on social media and those with whom you physically socialize. These individuals can inspire or influence you to do wonderful things. Or, influencers can negatively affect your life, particularly your financial life, by causing you to desire material things and spend money you don't have. Social media is a big reason why many of you fall victim to comparative influences.

Unlike the baby boomer and Gen X consumers who are influenced mostly by newspapers and television commercials, only 3% of millennials learn about products by watching TV or reading news magazines and other print media.[8] Many of you employ TiVo to skip annoying television commercials. Millennials rely more on blogs from your peers before making a purchase. You also take to social media to let your friends know your plans to buy a certain item and ask their opinion on the brands or features to consider. Word of mouth via social media is one of the most effective means of advertising. When you purchase something online, at the end of the ordering process, the merchant encourages you to Like and Share the news of your purchase with your friends. If you've purchased a popular and highly coveted item, you're more likely to Share.

Most of us seek approval and validation from others, particularly that of our peers. If our words say we don't seek validation, our behavior says otherwise, and marketers have caught on to this. Hence, the Share and the Like buttons. Using these buttons invite others in your community to validate your choices. Marketers benefit when your friends validate your choices by Liking or Sharing your post. Your friends begin receiving unsolicited advertisements in their News Feed from marketers pushing products like the ones you purchased. Marketers are experts at taking advantage of comparative influences. They're hoping your friends will be influenced to purchase the same or similar item. To illustrate the merits of social media validation, I'll share this story with you.

Several years ago, I decided to open a social media account. For Gen Xers or boomers, our first social media account is usually Facebook. My oldest millennial was fresh out of college and living at home to save money for her journey to independence. One evening I posted a status update that was very complimentary of my daughter. I expressed pride that she'd graduated college. The following morning, the first thing I did was check my status to see how many Likes and Comments I received overnight. There were a few of each, and I felt good about that. However, I didn't see a Like from my daughter. I walked to her bedroom and asked if she'd seen my post. She sleepily answered that she'd seen the post. It was obvious she was annoyed that I'd interrupted her sleep. I stood there for a moment unsatisfied with her answer. Sensing my presence, she opened her eyes with a puzzled look and asked, "What?" I replied with a question of my own, "So, why didn't you Like it?" She gave me one of those, "Really?" stares and pulled the covers over her head.

It was important to me that she acknowledged my posting on Facebook. I now admit that I wanted her to validate me publicly. It wasn't enough that I'd received a few Likes and Comments from others. But, the one person whose opinion mattered the most did not offer the public validation I desired. Later that morning, my daughter jokingly said to me, "Mom, you could have just told me in person. We live in the same house."

In the same manner, you and your friends may be seeking validation when posting on social media. When you post the very best of what's happening in your lives, you're hoping others Like it. This validation may cause you to continuously one-up yourself, which in turn may cause you to spend unnecessarily to keep up your "Likeability." Social media is the modern version of the elementary school event—Show & Tell. Show every detail of your vacation, to include pictures of your meals. The problem with Show & Tell posts is they can make you feel deprived if you have not yet learned the art of being content. How often can you see pictures of everyone's wonderful vacations, social events, cars, homes, clothing, and latest gadgets and not be enticed to long for those things? Never mind that you can't afford them. You may be genuinely happy for your friends or not care one way or the other, but the potential is there for you to feel jealous or inadequate.

The need to be validated and acknowledged can be so strong that people are going into debt trying to maintain an image of who they want people to think they are. The phrase "balling" comes to mind. I learned this term is used when referring to someone who appears to have a lot of money and living the good life— materialistically speaking. Referring to someone as a baller is considered a teasing compliment and it feeds into the brain's region for good feelings. It's gratifying when something gives you good feelings, and you want to experience that gratification as frequently as possible. Therefore, you continue the behaviors that generate those feelings. Posting the highlights of your baller life may yield several hundred Likes and Comments. I wonder what the response would be if you or your friends were required to include the amount of debt associated with that post. The caption on the post of a new luxury car would read, "Just got my dream car. Financed it for five years at 18% APR. #blessed."

Some people disguise their showboating by declaring their latest acquisition a blessing from God. While that may very well be the case, often they're simply boasting. Many of your friends' posts are staged to give viewers that perfect shot of their experience, which may not have been all that great. The need to create that perfect image is so great that even celebrities and models admit to staging their personal photos with rented vehicles or borrowed designer clothing for their Instagram photo posts.

Recognize this behavior for what it is and do not be tempted to feel jealous or feel that you lack because you don't have those things. *"One pretends to be rich, yet has nothing; another pretends to be poor, yet has great wealth."*[k] Some social media postings are the products of pretenders. Those who can truly afford the lifestyles portrayed don't waste time trying to impress others. They're too busy building their financial future instead of parading pretentiously in the present. I promise you, some of those pictures you see on social media are the cause of many people's financial struggles. The pictures of lavish meals and happy hour shenanigans come at a high cost like not being able to pay the rent or car payment. The truth is, many of your friends are not balling. Many of them have little to no savings and are behind in their student loan repayments. The reason some of them can indulge themselves in the "good life" is that they're still living with their parents and have yet to make real adult decisions for their future. Many of them are living paycheck to paycheck. Don't feed into the social media lies or get sidetracked by material deceitfulness. Do not allow social media to entice you to make purchases that are not in line with your financial goals. Learn to be content with what God has provided you thus far.

To be successful in planning your financial future, you must gain a different perspective on acquiring "things." Things do not define you as a person. Your value is not tied to the number and kinds of material things you have, nor is it measured by what others think is successful or attractive. God established your worth when He created you. *"For you formed my inward parts; you knitted me together in my mother's womb. I praise you, for I am fearfully and wonderfully made. Wonderful are your works; my soul knows it very well."*[1] Wow! God took the time to create you to be unique and complete in and of yourself and complete in Him. His work in creating you is perfect. Purchasing designer handbags, jewelry, or luxury vehicles cannot improve or add value to what God has created. You have got to get rid of stinking thinking. The need to look and be important through material acquisitions must not come at the sacrifice of your financial future. Don't go broke trying to establish an image to impress others.

Please don't misunderstand what I'm saying here. There is absolutely nothing wrong with wanting material things or wealth. It's your intentions that make the difference. Why do you want them? What purpose will they serve? Will they draw you closer to God or drive you further away? I've heard of numerous situations where individuals have prayed for a job making more money. They get the job, and the hours they're now required to work leaves very little time for their family, church, and ministry opportunities. But, they can now purchase a new luxury car and fabulous clothes. Who benefits here?

To keep yourself from having improper motives and longings for material things that cause you to go into or remain in debt, you must learn to be content. I understand you were taught that the sky is the limit. The world is your oyster. Aim high. And now, here comes some Gen Xer telling you just to be happy with where you are and what you have and call it a day. Not at all. Being satisfied or content simply means that you recognize your current state, but you also recognize the faithfulness of God. *"I know how to be brought low, and I know how to abound. In any and every circumstance, I have learned the secret of facing plenty and hunger, abundance and need. I can do all things through him who strengthens me."*[m]

If you're struggling financially and find it difficult to make sense of it all, God will give you strength to endure. That's not to say that you should sit idle. You should always make efforts to improve your situation. However, don't worry, complain, or otherwise be discontented while you're waiting for God's response. Be satisfied in knowing that He is aware of your needs and desires. He will always take care of you. As your desires line up with His will for your life, He will grant those to you as well. Therefore, being confident in this knowledge, there is no need for you to obsess over acquiring things or getting ahead. What He has for you will come in due time. God wants you to be financially successful. He wants you to have a lovely home, a nice car, and a healthy savings account.

God has two requirements of you—that you desire to know Him and follow his ways and that your blessings be used to bring Him glory. In other words, you should not fail to acknowledge the source of your blessings. In doing so, you point others to your source. Chris Brown, a pastor and public speaker who now partners in ministry with Dave Ramsey, wrote an article in which he stated, "Accumulating stuff just for the sake of stuff takes us down a dangerous road. When we keep our focus on God and use money for His glory, He blesses us with more."[9]

In your journey to financial freedom and wealth building, it is imperative that you remain diligent and conscientious of these barriers; lack of self-control, procrastination, and comparative influences. If you can overcome these three traps, you will be well on your way to living the life you were intended to live, stress-free and unburden by debt. You'll be able to build wealth, serve God with joy, and freely enjoy all that God has to offer.

* * *

1. Which of the three barriers to becoming financially healthy is most challenging for you? Self-control, procrastination, or comparative influences?

_____

_____

_____

_____

_____

2. What negative consequences have you experienced because of procrastination?

_____

_____

_____

_____

_____

CHAPTER 3

Credit 101

Desire without knowledge is not good, and whosoever
makes haste with his feet misses his way. (Proverbs 19:2)

A newly engaged couple is excited to open their first joint bank account. Their goals are to fund their wedding using cash and to save for a down payment on a home that they plan to purchase next year. The bank needed access to their credit reports to open the account. After reviewing the reports, the bank associate suggested they start working on improving their credit scores if they planned to buy a home. Both scores were in the 500s. After going home and discussing the bank visit, they Googled information on credit scores to learn the significance and ramifications of having scores in the 500s. Their excitement quickly turned to bewilderment. According to the leading credit scoring agency, their scores did not place them in the best position to meet their goal of acquiring a home loan. Although purchasing their home would not be impossible, the loan will cost more because higher interest rates are given to individuals with lower credit scores. Higher interest rates mean they'll have a higher monthly mortgage payment. A higher mortgage payment means they'll have less money to use towards other financial goals. They wondered how long their dream of buying a home would be delayed while they worked on cleaning up their credit. Unfortunately, their current situation began developing long before their visit to the bank.

Before they met, these 33 and 30-year-old millennials landed decent jobs after graduating from college and began repaying their student loans six months later. They began enjoying their lives by taking trips, shopping, routinely attending happy hours, and participating in other costly entertainment events. The idea of a spending plan or budget never crossed their minds. How do you think they funded their lifestyle? You guessed it. Credit cards.

As they tried to make good on the credit card payments, which were often late, the student loan payments became less of a priority. After multiple notices of past due letters from Sallie Mae, the loan servicing agency, they decided to call and make alternative payment arrangements. One requested lower payments and the other requested a hardship deferment. However, their procrastination in handling the matter sooner cost them a hit on their credit report. I'm certain that neither of them gave any thought to how their life-on-loan habits would affect their financial future. My goal in this chapter is to educate you on the basics of credit, how it works, and how the irresponsible use of credit impacts your ability to meet your financial goals.

Some individuals find themselves in dire financial situations simply because they aren't properly informed. When you don't understand how a process works, it can lead to undesirable consequences. Using credit is no different. You should know what those cards are costing you. You should know how much of your payments are going to the lender for their advanced generosity, also known as interest. And, you should know how much more you're paying for the privilege of being able to decrease your monthly student loan payments. Once you realize the ramifications, you'll try harder to make better choices. *"The prudent sees danger and hides himself, but the simple go on and suffer for it."*[a]

Many of you use credit cards regularly to purchase things you need. Some of you also purchase things, in excess, that you don't need. The generalization of millennials is that you want what you want, and you want it now. Some of you are racking up credit card debt like it's nobody's business with no concern or idea how you're going to pay it off. The good news is that it doesn't apply to all of you. According to an article in the New York Times, the percentage of millennials who have credit cards is at its lowest level since 1989. Sixty-three percent of you don't have a credit card.[1] Getting that first credit card may seem like a rite of passage, but not having one may prevent you from developing spending habits that lead to financial disaster.

There are several factors that prompted the decline in credit card usage among millennials. The Credit Card Act of 2009 changed the way credit card issuers reach out to college students. Credit card issuing companies used to set up tables at major college functions or in the busiest areas of campuses. This allowed students to trade their financial futures for a T-shirt or water bottle. A completed credit card application was all that was needed to be issued a credit card. It didn't matter that many of you were unemployed or underemployed with no ability to make credit card payments. The cards became another resource for funding college expenses and good times. It wasn't unusual for students to have graduated from college with multiple maxed out credit card balances. Without the ability to pay these debts, millennials left school with poor credit and mounting debt. With the passing of the

Credit Card Act of 2009, it is now a requirement that individuals applying for credit cards must prove they have income. As a result, the presence of college credit card predators has virtually disappeared.

Another factor contributing to the decline in credit card usage among millennials is that you witnessed first-hand the financial devastation left by the 2008 economic crisis. It's likely you or someone you know lost their job. Many of you couldn't find work. It certainly was no time to apply for credit cards. In other words, the economic crisis caused many of you to be scared straight. Even though millennials' use of credit cards has declined, a considerable number of you, 37%, *are* using credit cards to incur debt without understanding the ramifications of using the card irresponsibly. Based on my interactions with millennials, my guess would be that many of you don't understand the concept of credit at all, which renders you ill-equipped to use credit cards. In the world of personal finance, there are two popular thoughts when it comes to credit usage:

1. Never use credit cards.
2. Using credit cards is fine if you use them "wisely."

If you are using credit cards for virtually everything, not making timely payments, and carrying balances each month, my advice is that you stop using them immediately. Obviously, you haven't shown the discipline or knowledge to manage them properly. I hesitate to give exceptions because they tend to be interpreted loosely or stretched so far that they become excuses. But, my one exception to using credit cards is this: If you have mastered self-control *and* have consistently paid off the entire balance each consecutive month for at least one year, then you may be a candidate for using a credit card for perks like travel miles or the convenience of reserving cars and hotels. Make sure the cards do not have annual fees or other costs to use the card. I also advise that if you must have a credit card, use only one majorly accepted card—no retail store credit cards. The more credit cards you have, the more risks.

I realize some of you have already accumulated credit card debt and find it challenging to manage the payments. I'll discuss the best way to manage your credit card debt in the next chapter. For those of you who are contemplating applying for a credit card or have just begun to use them, my advice is that you pump the breaks. Do not apply for a credit card or use your credit card to purchase another item until you have finished reading this book.

Besides student loan debt, credit card usage is typically most millennials' introduction to debt. The line of credit offered to you (the maximum amount you can charge) is a "revolving" loan; it's open-ended and always available. Unlike other loans, the account doesn't close when you pay the balance. The line of credit remains available to create more debt. Some experts consider credit cards a tool of the devil whose sole mission is to destroy you financially. I don't think I'd take it that far. But, I have seen individuals whose lives were significantly changed for the worse due to the irresponsible use of credit cards.

When you borrow from the credit card issuer (by purchasing goods and services using their card), they are going to charge you interest. Credit card usage is the epitome of "pay to play." No one gives you a loan and not expect it to be repaid with interest except perhaps a relative or friend. If you choose to use a credit card, the way you manage the debt and repayments will impact your ability to meet other financial obligations. If you're spending a great portion of your income to pay credit card debt, you'll have less money available for other goals.

It is important that you manage credit wisely. How you manage your credit lets interested parties (banks, insurance agents, property managers) know:

- How creditworthy you are and if they can trust you to pay them back timely.

- The interest rates to charge you. The higher the risk, the higher the rate.

- Whether your application for an apartment rental or utilities will be approved, and if so, how much of a deposit you'll need to pay.

- How much your insurance company will cover on your properties (car and home).

- Whether you are employable.

Prospective employers cannot check your credit score, and they cannot access your full credit report or any information that's prohibited under equal employment opportunity laws. However, they can access information in your report that documents your payment history to your lenders. They may want to review this information to gauge your trustworthiness. Employers who are looking for the best staff may consider your report when deciding if you can be trusted to do your job responsibly. It's reported that 47% of employers check the credit history of prospective employees as a routine part of their hiring process.[2] One reason employers check credit history is that it decreases the likelihood of theft and embezzlement and reduces legal liability for negligent hiring. If your report has severe delinquencies, multiple judgments, liens, or bankruptcy, the company may not want to take a chance on hiring you. Information in your report might make you appear desperate for money. The implication is that you may be tempted to participate in shady behavior for personal gain during your employment.

Not all states allow employers to check credit reports, and state laws vary as to how the information is used. If you're concerned about this, research the laws in your state. Employers must have your written consent to check your credit history. Your reluctance to share this information may influence a company's hiring decision because it may appear that you have something to hide.

You might be asking on what basis these entities judge you. Well, in the world of credit, you are merely a number. Lenders don't care how many degrees you have, how active you are in church, or how many homeless or aging people you've served. And they certainly don't care how attractive you are. You are simply a number. Your number tells lenders all they need to know before deciding whether to loan you money. Your score is the lender's risk barometer.

CREDIT SCORES

There are many different scoring models in the industry and they all score a little differently. The most popular model is the FICO score. FICO is an acronym for Fair Isaac Co, a company that specializes in predictive analytics. FICO analyzes information to predict the likelihood that you will either stop paying your loan obligations or begin paying them in an unacceptable manner (late).

If you've built a reputation of paying your bills consistently on time, have very little debt, and carry small credit balances, your score will be on the higher end of the spectrum. On the other hand, if you have a poor history of meeting your payment obligations, your score will be on the lower end.

Credit scoring companies determine how much of a risk you are for borrowing money. FICO scores range from 300 to 850.[3] Lenders interpret these scores to mean the following:

800 or more: Scores in this range classify as Exceptional. If you're in this range, you shouldn't have any problems obtaining approval for a loan. There is only a 1 % chance that you will become delinquent in your obligation to pay the loan per the terms.

740 to 799: Scores in this range are considered Very Good. Although not as great as Exceptional, you can still feel good about this score because you'll qualify for better interest rates from lenders. I'll talk more about interest rates later in this chapter. FICO predicts that 2 % of you with credit scores in this range will probably become delinquent.

670 to 739: If your score falls within this range, you have a Good score. These scores are considered acceptable to lenders. However, your interest rates may not be the best, and you'll end up paying the lender more to use their money. FICO predicts that 8% of you with scores in this range will become delinquent.

580 to 669: Scores in this range are below average and are considered Fair. If your score is in this range, you are considered a subprime borrower. Subprime rates refer to the highest interest rates. A subprime lender is one who provides loans to people with poor credit, lower incomes, and insufficient documentation. Knowing these individuals pose a high risk of default, these lenders try to bleed borrowers for as much as they can through higher interest rates. By charging higher interest rates, the lender is maximizing recoupment of his money should the borrower defaults. If your credit score is in this range, know that interest rates will be astronomically high, which will make your loan extremely costly. Subprime lenders are opportunists who take advantage of people whose finances are already unhealthy. The borrower's credit history may include things, like collections, delinquent payment history, bankruptcy, foreclosure, charge-offs, etc. The prediction is that 28% of borrowers with scores in this range will become delinquent.

579 and lower: Credit scores in this range are considered Poor. If your FICO score falls within this range or even the Fair range, do not bother to apply for the loan. It is not a good idea for you or the lender. You will not qualify for mainstream loans, and you may be required to pay a deposit on utilities. These scores may be the result of bankruptcies, major credit card problems (overdue payments, frequently maxing out card limits, carrying large balances), and student loan defaults. A staggering 61 % of you with scores in this range are predicted to become delinquent on loan payments.

You may be wondering what makes up your score. Whenever you apply for credit, you provide personal information, like your name, social security number, birth date, and employment history. This information is reported to one or all three of the national credit bureaus, Experian, Equifax, and TransUnion. The personal information is used to properly identify you when your credit activity is reported. The bureaus consider several factors to come up with your credit score and your activity in these areas impact your credit score.

CREDIT SCORING

It is important to understand the factors that make up your credit score and how much weight is assigned to each factor. Knowing the breakdown is particularly helpful if you're working to improve your score because you'll know which areas require more attention. Below are the five factors that make up your credit score:

1. *Payment History* (35%) This factor is weighted by the number of times you make late payments. Do you consistently pay your bills on time? Defaults on installment loans (car, student, and mortgage debt) carry more weight than revolving loans (credit cards), but defaulting in either category affects your credit score.

2. *Credit Utilization* (30%) This area measures your percentage of available credit (sum of your credit limits) against the amount of credit being used (sum of your outstanding charges). If you have a $5,000 credit limit and your outstanding charges total $4,000, you're using 80% of your credit limit. This is not good and shows that you may not be handling credit responsibly. When you pay off a credit card, don't close the account. Cut the card up so that you're not tempted to use it. Leaving the account open gives you more "available" credit, which lowers your utilization rate. The lower your utilization percentage, the better. Zero is best!

3. *Age of credit history* (15%) The longer you have a credit account, the better off you are as it relates to scoring. A longer history gives a lender a better sense of your credit behavior. If you're new to credit, you may not gain any points here. However, this area is only 15% of the total score. NOTE: You don't need a credit card to build credit history. More on that later.

4. *New credit/inquiries* (10%) Lenders consider the number of credit accounts you open within a certain amount of time. If you are opening several accounts, like retail accounts, applying for a car loan, trying to get pre-approved for a home loan, or have frequent occurrences for either of these, this indicates you may be getting in over your head. If you're in the home-buying market and trying to get pre-approved for a home loan, realtors will caution you against applying for any credit. Resist the cashier who asks if you want to save an additional 20% on your purchase by applying for their store credit card. You should respond with a resolute "No thank you" for three reasons: 1) The 20% you saved is negated by the interest charged if you fail to pay your entire balance off at the end of the billing cycle, 2) You'll be enticed to buy more because of the special savings offered when using the card, and 3) You're adding to the number of inquiries on your credit.

When you apply for credit, the lender initiates an inquiry with one or all the credit reporting agencies. You've experienced this if you've ever applied for a department store credit card. It's important to know that businesses other than department stores are making credit inquiries. Apartment managers, insurance agents, and employers may also initiate inquiries. These kinds of inquiries are voluntary due to your request for credit, housing, or employment, and they impact your score. There are also non-voluntary inquiries resulting from lenders accessing your credit history to offer you credit. These inquiries do not impact your score. When you receive pre-approved credit card solicitations in your mailbox, consider them junk mail and throw them away immediately.

5. *Mix of accounts/types of credit* *(10%)* A mix of revolving and installment credit, like a credit card, car loan, student debt, and mortgage, is a factor that affects your score. Do not rush out and purposefully create the perfect mix. This opens the door for foolishness. Besides, the credit mix is only 10% of your score.

It's a good idea to review your credit report on a regular basis to monitor the activity. The reports often contain errors that may impact your scoring. By law, everyone is entitled to a free credit report each year from each of the three credit reporting agencies. You can obtain your reports at ***www.annualcreditreport.com***. If you find errors on your report, you must dispute the errors in writing directly to the agency. The instructions for disputing an entry or for correcting data are included with the report.

CREDIT CARD FEES AND INTEREST

Interest simply means additional money earned or paid. If you maintain a bank savings account with funds on deposit, you'll notice your account may earn extra money each month. Thanks to the impact of compounding, the longer you leave the money in the account, the faster it will grow. Each month, you'll earn interest on your balance, which includes the interest earned the previous month. Banks pay you for allowing them to use your money to issue loans to others and to make investments.

On the other hand, when the banks allow you to use *their* money by issuing you a credit card, they will charge fees and interest. Card issuers make billions of dollars a year collecting the following fees:

- Late fees now have a cap of $27 for a first-time offense and $38 for subsequent late payments thanks to the 2009 Credit Card Act. If you fail to pay your bill by the deadline, not only are you liable for the interest on the balance, you'll owe the late fee as well.

- Annual fees range from $25 to $195. This fee is charged each year just for the "privilege" of having the card. You've probably seen cards offered with no annual fees. They make up for this by charging higher interest rates and betting that you'll carry a balance and make late payments.

- Balance Transfer fees are typically 3% of the transfer amount. See Chapter Four for information on credit card balance transfers.

- Foreign transaction fees are about 3%. This fee is assessed on purchases you make with your card when you are out of the country.

- Cash advance fees are usually 5% of the cash amount borrowed or $10, whichever is greater. Don't do it. These are short term loans with high interest rates on top of the fees.

Interest seems to be the least understood for new and veteran cardholders. For those of you who have credit cards, have you ever read your credit card statement in its entirety? If so, you've probably noticed the interest rate you're charged. I'm going to ask that you stay with me on this because it is important that you know how your interest is calculated and how long you'll pay for those high fashion sunglasses or the got-to-have-it-now electronic device.

Credit card interest rates are described as the APR or annual percentage rate. This can be quite deceiving because no one charges interest on an annual basis. Interest is calculated daily using the DPR, or daily periodic rate. The APR must be converted into the DPR to get the actual amount of interest for the period. Some lenders include the DPR on their statements so it may not be necessary to do the conversion.

For example, let's say that at the beginning of the month your credit card balance is $400. On the 15th of the month, you charged a new state of the art TV for $1,100 bringing your total charges to $1,500. You made no other purchases during the month. Your average daily balance is calculated as follows:

($400*15 days) + ($1,500 *15 days) = $28,500/30 days in your billing cycle = $950

Your average daily balance for the period is $950.

Now, let's figure your daily periodic rate. Because you have a good FICO score, you were issued a card with an APR of 11%. The conversion to the DPR is as follows:

0.11 APR/365 calendar days = .00030 DPR (read your statement to find out if your card issuer uses a 360 or 365-day calendar)

The total interest for the month is calculated as follows:
$950 average daily balance *.00030 daily percentage rate *30 days = $8.59

Remember, your balance at the end of the billing cycle is $1,500. If you pay your balance in full by the due date, you'll owe no interest. However, if you let the balance roll forward, the following month's beginning balance will be $1,508.59.

Let's say you're now fed up with this debt and you decide you're not going to charge anything ever again. You decide to cut the card up and commit to paying the balance off. The chart below illustrates the effects of interest and how long it will take you to pay off a balance of $1,500 making various monthly payments. We'll assume the same APR of 11%:

Monthly Payment	Months to Pay Balance Off	Interest Paid	Total Paid
$30 (min)	68	$515.73	$2,015.73
$60	29	$211.54	$1,711.54
$100	17	$121.13	$1,621.13

If you pay the minimum amount due on this balance, it will take you 5 ½ years to pay off. Not to mention the amount of interest you'll pay. If you choose to use credit cards, you clearly see how important it is to charge only what you can afford to pay off at the end of the billing cycle. Carrying balances cost you more money and hinder your ability to meet other goals.

I took the time to go through the calculations above so you would understand the process. The Credit Card Act of 2009 requires that your credit card statement contains information telling you the number of months it would take you to pay the current balance if you make the minimum payment only. The statement also includes the total amount of interest you will have paid and the monthly payment required if you want to pay the balance in three years. Obviously, if you continue to add charges and pay the minimum amount due, it's going to cost you more and take you longer to pay off. Your statement must also list the toll-free number for you to call if you need information or counseling on debt management.

Many of you justify the use of credit cards as being a matter of convenience, a tool to help you build your credit history, and a means of racking up perks like frequent flier miles and rebates. The truth is, you don't need a credit card to build credit history and a great percentage of you never use the perks or recover the annual fees. Also, the monthly interest charges on your balances negate any perks you may have earned. For every perceived good reason to use credit cards, there is an offsetting bad reason.

PRO AND CONS OF CREDIT CARDS

The website, 360 Degrees-Financial Literacy, lists several pros and cons for using credit cards.[4] I've listed some of them below and included comments on the alternative approach of using debit cards:

Proponents of credit cards claim:

- Credit cards can save you time and trouble: no searching for an ATM or keeping cash on-hand.

- Low-cost loans: you can use credit cards to save today (e.g., one-day sales) when payday is a week away.

- Instant cash: cash advances are quick and convenient, putting cash in your hand when you need it.

- Perks: from frequent flier miles to discounts on automobiles, there is a program for everyone. Many credit card issuers offer incentive programs based on the dollar amount of your purchases.

- Builds positive credit: controlled use of a credit card can help you establish credit for the first time or rebuild credit if you've had problems in the past.

- Purchase and fraud protection: most credit card issuers will handle disputes for you. If a merchant won't allow you to return a defective product, or if fraudulent charges were made using your card, you can dispute those charges. The credit card issuer will provisionally remove those charges until an investigation is completed. At most, you may be liable for $50.

Opposers of credit cards claim:

- Overuse: revolving credit makes it easy to spend beyond your means because the card is open-ended. Once you pay the balance off, you can continue to purchase on the account.

- High-cost fees: your sale purchase will suddenly become much more expensive if you carry a balance or miss a payment.

- Unexpected fee: typically, you'll pay between two and four percent of the amount just to get the cash advance. Cash advances carry high interest rates.

- No free lunch: high interest rates and annual fees associated with credit cards often outweigh the perks.

- Deepening your debt: consumers are using credit more than ever before. If you charge freely, you will quickly find yourself in over your head.

- Homework: it's up to you to make sure you receive proper credit for incorrect or fraudulent charges.

Debit Card advantages:

- Convenient when you don't have cash--can't spend what you don't have. Subject to overdraft charges if you don't tell your bank to stop any transactions when there are insufficient funds.

- One-day-sales are no problem if you have the funds to buy. Chances are you don't need the item.

- Easy access to interest-free cash. It's your money, so it's free. Most point of sale transactions allow you to withdraw a limited amount of cash from your account.

- Banks are starting to offer some perks, but they are not as varied or as big as those offered by credit card issuers. Perks may include no-fee checking accounts and discounts at certain stores. However, the biggest perks are no monthly bill and no interest charges.

- Use has no impact on credit history.

I recently read an online article about Mark Cuban, the famously outspoken billionaire businessman who owns the Dallas Mavericks. He's also one of the sharks on the television show, "*Shark Tank*." In the article, Mark was asked to share his best money advice, which he said came from his dad. "Don't use credit cards." He claims that credit cards are the worst investments you can make. He goes on to say that the money he saves on interest by *not* having debt is better than any return he could get by investing in the stock market. Mark is not the only famous rich person who disdains credit cards. The article included Jay Leno, former host of *The Tonight Show*, as another hater of credit cards. "I don't carry any debt," he says. "I don't write checks at the end of the month for anything, and that includes my house. I didn't buy my house until I had cash. When you own something, and you don't have to write checks (or pay online) every month, you're just better off."[5]

I know you're probably thinking that these guys are rich, so it makes sense that they can afford to pay cash for everything. It may surprise you to know that both men are self-made, boot strap rich. They were not born into money, but they worked hard to become financially wealthy. The philosophy of paying cash and avoiding debt was great financial wisdom passed to them by their immigrant working middle-class parents. In fact, Jay Leno's mom was a homemaker who earned no money. I wanted to tell their stories because I want you to understand how the wisdom of the Bible is relevant in all eras, cultures, and all situations. It doesn't matter whether you have a little or a lot. There are certain principles to follow to be successful. The biblical principle of steering away from debt has obviously served Mark and Jay well.

You should feel more confident and better equipped to make wise decisions concerning the use of credit cards. Some personal financial advisors offer no other advice other than to warn you to stay away from credit cards altogether because of the pitfalls, and I certainly understand that position. However, credit cards are not the problem. It's the people who use the cards that need to change their behavior. I think it's great for those who choose not to expose themselves to the temptation. You should carefully weigh the costs and potential pitfalls against any perceived benefits. Those of you who are honest with yourselves know whether you have the self-control required to manage credit cards.

ALTERNATIVE METHODS FOR BUILDING CREDIT HISTORY

Contrary to popular beliefs, you do not need a credit card to build credit history. Consider the alternative methods below for building a healthy credit history without using credit cards:

1. Apply for a credit builder loan through your financial institution. These loan arrangements are designed specifically to assist people in building credit history. Most credit unions and some banks offer these loans. Apply for a small loan of $1,000 and deposit it into an interest-bearing account. Pay the loan off over the course of a year or two. Check with your banking institution to ensure your payments are reported to the three credit reporting agencies. Since you're building history, you want to make sure you start on a good footing by making your payments according to the terms of the loan. Or, better yet, pay the loan off early. Once you've paid the loan in full, the principal (amount borrowed) is turned over to you along with any interest earned.

2. If you have money in a savings account or a certificate of deposit, it can be used as security against a loan. The bank will loan you the amount of your savings and use your savings as collateral. Repay the loan according to

the loan terms. Request that the credit and payments be reported to the credit reporting agencies.

3. If you have a student loan, pay the agreed upon amount and pay it on time. These payments are automatically reported to the credit reporting agencies. The key is to pay consistently on time.

4. Personal loans are usually granted to individuals with sound employment. When I joined the Navy, I had no credit history. My mom wanted to purchase a home and needed assistance with the down payment. I applied for a signature loan with the credit union. Based on my employment, I was given a $2,000 loan. Combining the loan with my savings, I provided my mom the funds she needed. Although my loan terms gave me 24 months to repay the loan, I promptly repaid the loan in full within one year. The goal with any debt is to get rid of it as quickly as possible.

5. Apartment rental payments, which are not typically included in your credit score, may appear on your credit report. Potential employers and utility companies may view your report to see if you consistently pay your obligations timely before hiring you or waiving deposits. You should check with your property manager to ensure your payments are being reported to the credit reporting agencies.

6. Finance a small item through a retailer who offers installment loans. This will not only add to your credit history but also to your credit mix. Furniture stores are great at offering installment loans through their partner

financing companies. Usually, the only qualifying requirement is that you are gainfully employed. Remember, the objective is to build credit—not to furnish your entire apartment on installment. I suggest you finance up to what you can afford to pay in cash. Make sure the retailer is offering a no-interest deal for a certain number of months. Plan to pay the loan back over the course of the no-interest period. It's important that you stay aware of the no-interest expiration date. If you don't pay the loan off by the end of the period, the very next bill will include all the interest accumulated from day one of the loan. Paying off your installment loan earlier than the terms looks great on your credit report.

7. Become an authorized user. If you have a relative with excellent credit habits and who trusts you, they can add you to one of their accounts as an authorized user. They don't even have to give you a card or the account number, and you don't have to use the account. Any activity on that account will also reflect on your credit history. After a year, your name can be removed from the account.

These are all viable alternatives to building credit history without getting into the credit card business. Consider the many options and determine which option is best for you to establish or rebuild credit. You should think long and hard about assuming credit cards. Take a self-inventory to determine why you feel it necessary to have one. If you already have one or more cards and find yourself in a high debt situation, you should immediately stop using the cards and begin a debt elimination plan to get out of the credit business once and for all.

When you enter debt, you are assuming to know the future because you're counting on being able to make future payments to pay the debt. *Come now, you who say, "Today or tomorrow we will go into such and such a town and spend a year there and trade and make a profit," yet you do not know what tomorrow will bring. What is your life? For you are a mist that appears for a little time and then vanishes."*[b] You may encounter a financial crisis like a job loss or some other event that causes your income to decrease. It will be difficult to meet your credit card debt obligations. Credit card debt also insinuates that you are not trusting God to provide for you. God will meet your needs and bless you with your desires, and it won't require you to go into debt. It may require you to be patient or come up with a way to make additional income. Or, he may bless you through others. God's ways are not your ways. He wants to bless you, but He also wants to do it His way. If He does it His way, you can rest assured it's the best way. Don't borrow your blessings.

If you choose to use credit, consider the wisdom of King Solomon in the Bible. *"The rich rules over the poor and the borrower is the slave of the lender."* [c] The Life Application Bible[5] explains it this way; we are not forbidden to borrow, but we are warned to never take on a loan without carefully examining our ability to repay it. This not only applies to your finances but in every area of your life. You must consider the cost of your decisions. What may seem like a great idea may turn out to be the worst possible thing simply because you failed to practice self-control, use wisdom, and pray for guidance.

Being a member of the smartest generation ever, and now having gained more knowledge of credit, I'm confident you will make a wise choice. If you're already using credit cards and find yourself caught in a trap, beating yourself up will not improve the situation. The first step to fixing your credit problem is committing to change your behavior. The next step is cutting the credit cards in half. Do not use them from this point forward. Be encouraged. It's all good even if it doesn't look good. The fact that you're reading this book and deciding to commit to the process makes it better than good. It's great!

* * *

1. If you use credit cards, would you say that you use them responsibly, and what does that look like?

_____

_____

_____

_____

_____

2. Why do you think it's necessary for credit card statements to include the telephone number for debt counseling?

_____

_____

_____

_____

_____

CHAPTER 4

Deciphering Debt, Part I

*The rich rules over the poor, and the borrower is
a slave of the lender.* (Proverbs 22:7)

W hen it comes to American culture, accumulating debt is as common as baseball and apple pie. It's just what we do. We do debt. From credit card to automobile, education, and mortgage debt, we are accustomed to buying now and paying later. You can't log on to the Internet without being bombarded with ads offering 0% interest on a credit card. Many of you see these offerings as the answer to getting the things you want. We're a nation of consumers at the mercy of marketing experts who are trained to make us believe that we need *things* to make us happier, slimmer, more beautiful, and accepted. We're made to feel as if we are somehow lacking if we don't buy the products the advertisers are pushing. We're convinced that we need to upgrade our homes, clothes, and gadgets because if we don't keep up with the latest versions, what will people think?

The need to have the latest and to be the first to get it is evident in the behavior of those who spend hours, and sometimes days, waiting in line for the release of the next generation of the iPhone or celebrity sneakers. An article on USA Today.com reported that most millennials (67%) have less than $1,000 in savings.[1]

Unfortunately, many of you are going into debt for the bragging rights of being the first to have a gadget. It stands to reason that some of you are not able to save because your money is held hostage by debt created from purchasing the latest things.

Recently, I was speaking with a young man who is friends with my millennial son, Keith. The man is a 26-years-old, single, college graduate with no children and an annual salary of about $40,000. Less than a year ago, he purchased a townhome. He's also financing a three-year-old used luxury car that he purchased last year. The car is in great shape. He has a consolidated student loan payment that he recently arranged for income-based payments. Lastly, he has credit card debt to the tune of $6,000.

During our conversation, he mentioned that he wants to upgrade his vehicle by purchasing a brand new one. Of course, my fiscally responsible antenna sensed something very wrong with his announcement. Before I realized it, I began firing off several questions allowing no time for his responses. "Don't you realize you're going to have a higher car payment? How much do you owe on your current car? What about your credit card balance? What about your student loan payments? Why do you want to go further into debt? Why don't you wait and pay down your loans? Do you know what you're doing?" After staring at me with a look of bewilderment, he shook his head and walked away saying, "Geesh! Now I understand what Keith goes through."

I don't know what comes over me when I hear this kind of talk from millennials. I seem to take it very personally as if it's my job to save every millennial from financial ruin. I know you're not intentionally sabotaging your financial future. You simply have not been taught to manage or avoid debt. Many of you think that if you make enough money to cover your bills, there's no problem. The problem is that it's not okay just being able to cover your bills. What about your future wealth, goals, and dreams? What about being able to help others? Tying all your money up in debt payments pretty much guarantees that you'll be challenged to manage life events that require financial resources. Although carrying debt seems to be the norm, it is not wise. Being wise means that you count the cost up front and make purchasing decisions based on current resources. Having to direct your income to debt payments limits your ability to serve and give generously in a manner that brings honor to God and blessings to you and your family. If you want to build wealth and meet financial goals, going into more debt is not the way to get there. The debt that challenges most millennials is student loan debt, so let's start the discussion there.

STUDENT LOAN DEBT

During the 2016 presidential campaign, one candidate clearly stood out among millennial voters—Bernie Sanders. Millennials viewed Bernie as an honest, authentic, and progressive man who understood your struggles and concerns. One major issue that threatens to delay your upward economic mobility is the student debt crisis. Bernie got it. He knew the trickle-down effect of so many young people being burdened by what seems to be insurmountable student loan debt. How can millennials, as America's largest generation, contribute economically to society if you can't purchase homes, start small businesses, get married, start families, save for retirement or other things that keep the economic wheels rolling? Considering that it typically takes ten or more years to pay off student loan debt, millennials are far behind previous generations in realizing their dreams. Bernie made student loan debt and the astronomical costs of college a major talking point of his campaign. Unfortunately, the tide was not in Bernie's favor. Although he did not win his party's nomination, he started a real conversation about the student debt crisis and the need for reform and relief.

Americans owe $1.3 trillion in student debt, which represents 6% of the overall national debt. Forty percent of that debt is attributed to graduate students.[1] Consider the following:

- The average 2016 graduate had $37,172 in student debt

- 43 million people have outstanding student loans (43% of those are behind in payments)

- The delinquency rate is 11.6% (90 days or more overdue)

- $351 is the average monthly payment of millennial student loans

- The average time it takes to pay off a student loan debt is ten years

With these mortifying statistics, it is unfortunate that many of you do not fully understand how the student loan process works or the ramifications of acquiring and mismanaging such debt. Failing to give student loan debt the attention it warrants and procrastinating on making payments or arrangements with the loan servicing agencies will not make it go away. Even the most recent college graduates are not educated about their debt and seem to be purposely ignoring the importance of repaying the loan. Citizens Bank confirmed what I already knew to be true based on my observations of how my daughter managed her student loans.[2] The survey found:

- 45% of survey respondents didn't know what percentage of their salary went to paying off their loans

- 37% were unaware of the interest rate on their loan

- 15% were unaware of how much they owe

- 44% do not fully understand the difference between federal and private loans

- 57% of millennial borrowers say they regret the amount of money they borrowed

- 33% of borrowers say they would not have gone to college had they realized the true price tag

The saddest of these statistics is the 33% of you who said you would not have gone to college had you known what it would cost. Unfortunately, the costs extend far beyond the expenses of college. There is the continuing cost of how your life is financially impacted for many years afterward. Anyone who wants to go to college should not be discouraged by the cost. The affordability of college must be addressed at the federal level.

You can't afford to be complacent carrying student loan debt. In fact, it should make you very uncomfortable. I don't mean to imply that you should be overly stressed, but there should be an elevated level of concern because of the impact on your future. The Citizen's Bank survey revealed that paying off student loan debt does not appear to be a priority. Less than 50% of those with student loan debt admitted they would not be willing to give up concert tickets, lattes, traveling, alcohol, or food deliveries to eliminate their student loan debt. If you have $37,000 in debt and it's going to take you ten years to eliminate, I agree that it may not be realistic to think that you won't buy a latte or eat takeout pizza for the duration. But, if you're serious about getting rid of this debt as quickly as possible, you're going to have to adjust your spending priorities and decide what sacrifices you *are* willing to make.

If you haven't been managing your student loan debt properly, now is the time to decide that you will no longer be a slave to the lender and that you're going to free yourself from the limitations this debt places on your life. The worst part of being a slave to debt is that you become so accustomed to it, that you don't even realize it's sucking the life right out of your future. You may have what you think are legitimate reasons, like unemployment or underemployment, for not attacking your loan repayments intensely. However, far too many of you have taken a lackadaisical attitude towards repayment of your loans. It stops now.

Knowing what you're dealing with is the first step in attacking the debt. Make it a point to understand the type of loan you have, interest rates charged, and how long you'll be making monthly payments. You should know whether you have federal loans or private loans. Federal loans are subsidized or guaranteed by the government. The interest rates are typically much lower compared to private loans, and the ramifications of delinquent and defaulted loans differ. If you're struggling to pay your student loans, please take the following advice very seriously.

Options for Late or Missed Payments

As soon as you know your payment will be late or that you'll miss a payment, contact your loan servicer. Your loan servicer is the entity that manages federally guaranteed student loans. They bill you, contact you when you're late, handle collections, and work with you when you're experiencing challenges meeting repayment obligations. The most popular loan servicer is Navient. You may be more familiar with the former name, Sallie Mae.

Once you reach out to the loan servicer and communicate your circumstance, you may be presented several loan management options, including deferment, forbearance, extended payments, income contingent plans, and forgiveness (a very rare and difficult option to obtain). Below is a summary of the four loan management options you may be offered:[3,4]

1. *Change your payment due date.* If you have difficulty putting money aside for your payment so that it's available when your payment is due, the loan servicer will work with you to arrange a payment due date that coincides with your salary payday. You can also authorize your loan servicer to debit your account on your payday or another day that fits your cashflow schedule. Additionally, you can arrange for a payroll allotment or direct deposit of the amount due, so the funds go directly to the loan servicer. This is a fantastic way to avoid the temptation to use the money for some other purpose.

2. *Change your payment plan.* If you are on the standard repayment plan that entails paying a designated amount each month for the duration of the loan (usually ten years), and the amount of your monthly payment is causing you financial distress, speak to your loan servicer about other repayment plans:

- *Extended Repayment Plan*: This plan is for those with more than $30,000 in total student loans and can last 25 years. Payments can be fixed, as with the standard plan, or graduated. Caution: In either case, you will end up paying much more for the loan. Because payments are stretched out longer, you'll end up paying significantly more in interest.

- *Income Driven Repayment Plans*: There are several options that will allow your payments to be calculated based on a percentage of your income, typically 10% to 15% of discretionary income. The payment amount will fluctuate based on your income (including your spouse's income if you file taxes jointly) and family size. There may be an option for loan forgiveness after 20 to 25 years depending on the type of loan you have.

- *Graduated Repayment Plans*: This plan assumes your income will steadily increase over time. Payments start out small and gradually increase every two years. The term is usually up to 10 years but may be longer for consolidated loans. Again, the total cost of the loan is significantly higher than the standard repayment plan because of additional interest.

I recommend you try sticking with the standard repayment plan making whatever sacrifices necessary to pay it off as quickly as possible. If you cannot make the payments under the standard plan and anticipate earning more money over the next ten years, the graduated repayment plan may be an option.

3. Deferment. A period where you're allowed to suspend your payments is called deferment. Unlike some other delayed or postponed loan payment terms, the interest does not accrue (add up) during this period. Your payments take a pause and then resume at the agreed upon time. Deferments may be granted for reasons, like education continuances, temporary trouble in making payments, unemployment, and economic hardship. Of course, deferments increase the amount of time you remain in debt.

4. Forbearance. As with deferment, forbearance also suspends your payments. But, unlike deferment, the interest continues to accrue. If you fail to pay the interest, it may be added to the principal, and you'll end up paying interest on the interest. If possible, try to avoid forbearance. Loan servicers will push this option because it's profitable for them. When you call, you are likely to hear this: "So, you want to put your payments on hold for about a year? Sure, no problem, we'll get that set up for you right away. We're so happy to be able to help you." But, what they are really saying is, "Oh, you want to give us extra money? We appreciate you for making us richer because we can't possibly have enough money." When you choose the option of forbearance to manage your loan payments, you are offering the lender more money to allow you to stay in debt for a longer period. That just doesn't make sense.

Options for Resolving Defaulted Loans

If you fail to make payments on time or miss payments, your loan will become delinquent. If it remains in a delinquent status for 270 days, the loan then goes into default. While the loan is delinquent, you may still work with the loan servicer to come up with a more suitable repayment plan. Late or missed payments will be reported on your credit report and affect your credit score.

If your loan goes into default, you may experience the following consequences:[4]

- The entire balance of the loan may become due and payable immediately.

- You will not be eligible for traditional repayment options or additional student aid.

- Your account may be referred to a collection agency.

- The debt will increase because of the late fees, additional interest, court costs, collection fees, attorney's fees, and any other costs associated with the collection process.

- The default will be reported to credit bureaus and impact your credit score.

- The IRS can take any federal and state tax return due to you and apply it to your debt.

- Your employer may be ordered by the federal government to withhold a portion of your pay and apply it to the loan (wage garnishment).

To illustrate the impact of a default, let's say your loan balance is $30,000. Adding the interest due at the time of your default and assuming 5% interest, this increases the balance by $1,500 to $31,500. When we include the average collection cost of 25%, an additional $7,500 is added. Your $30,000 loan now has a balance of $39,000 payable immediately. And this does not include any fees that may have been assessed along the way. This will never make sense to me. If you can't pay the original amount, surely you can't pay the additional interest and fees. This is capitalistic greed at its worst!

I'm reminded of a time when I was teaching a lesson on forgiveness to a group of middle schoolers. The lesson was from Matthew 18: 21-35, where Jesus was telling a parable about a servant who owed a debt to his master and was unable to pay. The master proceeds to choke the servant while demanding payment. As the servant begged for mercy, the master threw him in jail until he could pay the debt. As I finished reading the parable, a young student raised her hand and innocently asked, "How is the servant going to pay the master back if he's in jail?"

This is the same thought I have for millennials who feel imprisoned with the pressures of paying student loans while trying to make a life. Just like the servant who was thrown into jail and can't pay his debt until released, many of you can't realize your dreams until you are "released" from your student loan debt. You may feel that the only alternative to moving on with your life is to go further into debt. I am telling you--more debt is not the answer.

If your loan is already in default, contact the Department of Education. You'll be assigned to a case manager who will guide you through the process of getting out of default. I encourage you to work resolutely with your case manager to decide which of the following three options is best for your situation.

*1. **Immediate settlement of the debt.*** The option to settle the debt immediately is not usually exercised by many of you. If the loan is in default, it's not likely you'll have the full amount at once. However, if you have a smaller balance, you may be able to settle the debt quickly by selling some of your possessions, like a car, furniture, jewelry, or other items of value. One advantage of being able to settle immediately is that additional interest and fees may be waived, which in the earlier example would save you $9,000. Consider allowing others to gift you with cash. You'd be surprised by the number of people who may help if they see you making sacrifices to work it out yourself. But, if they see you living a baller's life, they may not be so inclined to help.

*2. **Loan Rehabilitation.*** This is a one-time deal where you agree to make payments under strict guidelines for nine months over a 10-month period. Your loan is considered rehabilitated after you have made the required payments. A loan rehabilitation removes your loan from default status, and the credit reporting agencies will remove the default from your credit history. However, any delinquent payments reported before the default will remain in your credit history.

*3. **Loan Consolidation.*** This option allows you to consolidate multiple student loans into one Direct Consolidation Loan with a fixed interest rate. You must agree to pay the consolidated loan under an income-driven repayment plan, or you can make three full, consecutive, and on time payments *before* you consolidate. Unlike rehabilitation, the default will not be removed from your credit history.

The Bible admonishes that we should avoid debt. If we enter debt, we are obligated to repay. In some instances, debt may be forgiven as illustrated in the parable mentioned earlier (Matthew 18:21-35). In like manner, there are provisions for student loan debt to be discharged through forgiveness, cancellation, or bankruptcy. There are very strict qualifications for loan discharges, and not all loan types qualify for all types of discharges. Below is a condensed list of qualifying criteria for discharges:

- Closed School Discharge (applies to you if your school closed while you were enrolled)

- False Certification of Student Eligibility (the school made false statements to qualify you for aid) or Unauthorized Payment Discharged

- Unpaid Refund Discharge (withdrew from school but did not receive a refund)

- Teacher Loan Forgiveness (after five years of teaching in a low-income school)

- Public Service Loan Forgiveness (remaining balances are forgiven for working in certain government entities at the federal, state, or local level)

- Total and Permanent Disability (TPD) Discharge

- Death Discharge

- Bankruptcy Discharge (should only be considered if there are circumstances beyond your control, such as a disability that renders you unable to acquire income to provide for your basic needs).

For more information on discharges, visit **www.studentloans.gov**.[4]

The options discussed above refer to student loans backed by the federal government. Private loans have their own rules, and lenders may treat delinquent payments and defaults differently. If you have a private student loan and have difficulty making your payments, contact your lender immediately to communicate your situation and ask about relief options.

When I look at the heavy burden of penalties placed on student loan borrowers, I wonder who we have become as a nation as it relates to educating our citizens. The runaway cost of college, the greed of the lenders, and the naivety of 18-year old borrowers signing their lives away are economic and social problems for us all. Even though it seems the system is stacked against you, you still have an obligation to pay the debt you owe as quickly as possible. *"Free yourself, like a gazelle from the hand of the hunter…"*[a] A gazelle is an animal that struggles fiercely to free itself when apprehended. It's also very swift and fast, which allows it to escape from danger. To borrow a phrase from Dave Ramsey, you must be "gazelle intense" in freeing yourself from student loan debt. Use all your power and might to loosen the chokehold this debt has on your life. And be swift and fast about it. The sooner you're free, the sooner you can get on with your life.

If you're making your monthly student loan payments and it's not causing you any real financial stress, great. What more can you do to pay the debt off even faster? Find ways to throw as much money as you can towards that balance. If you find yourself discouraged as you work through this debt, I encourage you to view testimonies of other millennials who have successfully eliminated their student loan debt in minimal time. Google or search YouTube using, "How I paid off my student loans," and you will get a plethora of videos with testimonials and suggestions on how you too can be successful in paying these loans off early.

Even though the millennials in the videos took slightly different approaches, there are three actions reflected in their stories that are critical to your success:

1. You must be intentional. Be on a serious mission with a purpose and a foreseeable destination.

2. You must make "temporary" sacrifices. Don't be afraid to adjust everyday indulgences. Sell some stuff or get a second job. Do whatever you legally and morally can do to raise money to pay your debt. Remember, it is only temporary.

3. You must be committed. Settle it in your mind and heart that you are going to see the process through to the end no matter what.

If you have no student loans and are thinking about funding your education through loans, you should seriously reconsider and look for other options. Borrowing for school without any idea how you're going to repay the loan is a gamble. You don't know what your financial situation will be after graduating. Remember, before going into debt you must count the cost and have a plan to repay the loan.

So, what *should* you do if you want to go to college without signing your life away on student loans? The short answers are, work hard and make sacrifices. You must re-evaluate your priorities and the value you place on things. You may face criticism and pressure from peers for the sacrifices you make, like living at home with your parents or passing up on vacations and happy hour.

There are other options for funding your education besides loans. These options require you to practice delaying gratification and exercise self-control. Keep your eyes on the prize. Your reward will be walking away with your degree or certification and realizing that your walk is much lighter and your future much brighter because you don't have to deal with the burden of student loan debt. Below are six options you should consider as alternatives to student loans.

ALTERNATIVE OPTIONS FOR FUNDING COLLEGE

Consider your school choices. Many students choose to attend a traditional four-year school based on its popularity, distance from their parents, social amenities, or because they want to experience the "true" college experience without considering or caring about the cost. If you choose a traditional school, consider enrolling in community college for the first two years. The tuition is significantly less compared to a four-year school. In most cases, there's an option to transfer to a traditional four-year school. Community colleges offer a quality education at a reasonable cost. They may lack the perceived prestige and social life of the bigger universities, but in the bigger scheme of life, how important is that to you? Do you want to spend the next ten or more years of your life paying off student loan debt simply for the "college experience?" I doubt you'll be smiling and reminiscing about your good old college days when you're making your monthly student loan payments.

Perhaps you don't need to attend a traditional two or four-year collegiate program. If you don't want to spend a lot of time or money taking courses that may not be directly relevant to your career choice, look for programs at trade (aka career or technical) schools. Traditional colleges and universities require you to take additional liberal arts classes designed to produce a better-rounded graduate. However, there's no need to spend money on these classes if you're interested in a trade career, like computer programming, multi-media art, or dental hygiene, which all pay a median salary of $65,000. If a career school offers what you want, why not spend two years or less training, and then start your career immediately? These educational opportunities are less of a financial burden and put you that much closer to your goals, preferably debt free. While your traditional school colleagues are graduating and attempting to look for jobs, you're already two years ahead of the game with money to start building your wealth and reaching your financial goals.

In addition to choosing the right school, you should carefully consider your field of study. The plan is for you to be financially independent upon graduation. Don't major in a field where the job market does not pay you enough to afford a place to live or make other adult moves. If your desire is to make a salary of $75,000, you may not want to major in elementary education. On the other hand, if teaching kindergarten is your calling, then you should be content with the lifestyle commensurate with a teacher's salary.

Work first, study later. Delay college until you have the money. It may be difficult watching your friends go off to college. I cannot stress enough the importance of practicing delayed gratification, ignoring the influence of others, and focusing on the bigger picture of being debt free upon graduation. You've got to make decisions that place you in the best position to meet your goals. One suggestion is to get a full-time job for a year while saving as much money as you can towards a full year of tuition. This will allow you to focus on your first year of school and not worry about money. Continue to work full-time during the summers. After the first year of school, you should have acclimated yourself to the rigors of college and should be able to work part-time while going to school, paying your expenses as you go. It's going to be very tempting to spend the summers traveling as opposed to working. Remember, this is a temporary sacrifice.

Work while attending school. This requires you to have good organizational and time management skills so that you stay on top of your course work. The optimum situation would be to land a job with an employer who contributes to the funding of your education. Many companies have employee tuition reimbursement programs. The reimbursements are per class so you can take as many as you can afford. If it takes you longer to finish, so what? It's time well spent. In addition to getting paid, you'll gain work experience and make professional contacts. Landing a job at a college or university is an ideal situation. As an employee, most colleges will allow you to take courses for little or no costs.

Check out the job recruitment website indeed.com. The site allows you to search companies by different criteria. Search for jobs that offer tuition reimbursement. The job you apply for may not be your dream job but look at it as simply a means to an end. Your objectives are to work, save money, and get through school. Visit Indeed.com to view jobs in your area.[5]

Live at home or with a roommate. The biggest college expense is room and board. With 36% of millennials now living at home with their parents, the stigma attached to this living arrangement has virtually disappeared.[10] Living at home will dramatically cut your expenses and allow you to fund your college education more easily. Most parents are willing to allow you to live with them if you're using your income for your education. If your parents are gracious enough to allow you this type of living arrangement, don't take advantage of their kindness. Show gratitude by doing your part to help keep the home running smoothly. Washing dishes or taking the trash out without being asked will go a long way.

Take Online Courses. Online degree programs and individual classes are significantly less expensive than programs at brick and mortar institutions. With online programs, you'll eliminate the cost of room and board and transportation. The beauty of online programs is that you can take them anywhere there is access to a computer and the Internet. You'll never have to worry about 'missing' class due to work or family obligations. Online programs have most of the same concentrations as brick and mortar schools and the degrees awarded carry the same weight. I've had millennial staff who continued their education online while working full time. They seemed to be content pursuing their degree while eating lunch.

I've heard millennials voice concern about not having the discipline to take online courses because they feel they'd have too many distractions. I suggest that before you rule out an online education, try at least one class to determine if it fits your learning style. Before selecting an online school, make sure the school is regionally accredited.

Research scholarships and grants. You'll be surprised how many different scholarships and grants are available. Apply for anything for which you might be eligible. There are scholarships based on ethnicity, military service, specific fields of study, etc. As I was researching this topic, I discovered a "Don't Text and Drive Scholarship" for $1,000, and the only requirement is to write a 500 to 1,000-word essay. If you're going to a community college, $1,000 will make a huge dent in your costs. To search for scholarships and grants, visit **www.scholarships.com**, or **www.fastweb.com**.

Military Service. If you choose to serve the country, you will have access to a free college education. All branches of the military, including the National Guard and Reserves, offer a variety of tuition assistance programs. The eligibility criteria may be different for each branch of service. For more information on the programs listed below, visit **www.military.com**:

- Armed Forces Tuition Assistance: Allows active duty and reserve members to have 100% of their college tuition and fees paid. The Coast Guard allows 75%. The Marines allow active duty members only to participate.

- Post-9/11 GI Bill: Allows military members who served a minimum of 90 days active duty since September 11, 2001, to have 40% to 100% of tuition and fees paid.

- Montgomery GI Bill: Service members enroll in the program and pay $100 per month for a year. In turn, they receive a monthly benefit for educational expenses, as much as $1,500 in some cases.

- Reserved Officers' Training Corps (ROTC): Civilian college students may participate in this military leadership program while attending college. In some cases, they receive a full scholarship in exchange for a commitment to serve as an officer in one of the military branches for a certain number of years.

One of the challenges millennials face when entering the workforce is a lack of job experience or lack of a degree. The military offers the opportunity to gain both with minimal or no cost. In addition to having the opportunity to serve the country, the military offers career training in almost every major concentration offered by colleges and trade schools, like finance, nursing, dentistry, human resources, air traffic control, photography, culinary science, computer information systems and others. If you choose to enlist in the military, once your obligated service is over, you will be a triple threat in the workforce. You will have gained experience, education, and you'll have veteran status. These three things combined should give you a significant edge over most job candidates.

* * *

1. If you have student loan balances, what practical steps can you take to pay your loan balances faster?

_____

_____

_____

_____

2. How would you advise a younger millennial who is considering using student loans to fund their college education?

_____

_____

_____

_____

CHAPTER 5

Deciphering Debt, Part II

Owe no one anything, except to love each other,
for the one who loves another has fulfilled the law
(Romans 13:8)

Because of long-term ramifications, debt is something that I really want you to wrap your mind around. If you understand how the various aspects of debt work, you're more likely to avoid getting deeply involved. This chapter continues the debt conversation with three more prevalent sources; consumer, payday, and mortgage loans.

CONSUMER DEBT

As mentioned earlier, the recession of 2008 left many of you resigned to taking whatever jobs you could find just to pay your bills, and many of you turned to credit cards to make ends meet. I know first-hand the struggles millennials experienced during this period. As a Sunday School teacher, I hear many stories of young people dealing with employment issues. It seems most everyone is looking and praying for a job or looking for a better job. During the recession, employers were forced with the decision to hire fresh-faced, younger millennials or over-qualified mature workers with families to support. Both candidates were seeking entry-level positions. Millennials took jobs unrelated to their college majors. My daughter graduated from college in 2009 as an English major and took a job as a cashier at a home improvement store before landing a teaching job.

Many of you began purchasing everyday necessities in addition to other nonessential items using credit. These credit card purchases consisted of goods that were consumable or had no value of appreciation. As opposed to investment debt, credit card debt is considered consumer debt. According to a 2016 report by ValuePenguin, credit card consumer debt is $929 billion. Thirty-eight percent of all households have some credit card debt, and the average balance is $16,048 per household. And get this: Households with the lowest or negative net worth have the highest debt.[1] In other words, individuals who can least afford to pay their credit card bills have racked up the most debt. When it comes to millennials, the good news is that Federal Reserve data shows that consumer debt for millennials is at its lowest since 1989. Fortunately, more of you are opting to use debit cards and are not as eager to be in the kind of consumer debt your parents assumed.[2] Even so, for those of you who are using credit, a whopping 43% of you have credit scores less than 600,[3] which indicates you are not managing debt wisely.

PAYDAY AND TITLE LOAN DEBT

Payday loans or Title loans, also known as Quickie loans, should be avoided at all cost. These high-fee, short-term installment loans are a trap. The establishments are located mostly in communities of low-income wage earners but are becoming popular in suburbia where incomes are typically higher. These lenders were virtually nonexistent in 2004. However, by 2014 there were more payday lending establishments than McDonald's restaurants![4] Payday lenders have a reputation for taking advantage of those who can least afford to repay the loans, and many borrowers end up in far worse shape. A recent study revealed that 34% of millennials across socioeconomic lines had used payday lenders or pawn shops for quick access to cash. Your use can be attributed to lack of financial literacy and lack of savings.[5] There typically is no credit check, and all that's required to get a payday loan is a bank account and a job. Let's look at Sam's situation to illustrate how most payday loans work:

Sam lives in Florida and manages to get by living paycheck to paycheck. He makes enough money to cover his necessities. He has a banking account because his job requires that his pay is directly deposited. Sam has poor credit, partially due to defaulting on a car loan. He does not own a credit card. Sam is paid every two weeks. He received a phone call informing him that a close relative has passed away, and the funeral service will be held in California in two days. Sam wants to go to the service and needs to purchase a plane ticket. However, he doesn't get paid for another week. Sam goes to a payday loan business and receives a cash advance of $500 and is charged $15 for every $100 borrowed, which means he must repay $575. Sam's APR is 391% for the $500 loan. The average credit card interest rate is about 18%.

When Sam returned to Florida, he realized he didn't have enough money to pay his utility bills, and he'll be short on his rent because of the $575 he must repay. He arranges for the loan to roll over, which means the time to repay the loan is extended for an additional charge of $75. Sam now owes $650. This is why I call these loans traps. If Sam can't afford to repay the original $500, where is he going to get $650? This industry makes $46 billion by charging huge fees and interest rates to the most financially vulnerable populations all in the name of greed.[6]

The good news is that those who use payday loans may soon be getting help. The Consumer Financial Protection Bureau proposed regulations that attempt to mitigate the potential hardship placed on borrowers. Four of the proposed changes are:[7]

- Lenders will be required to establish a borrower's ability to repay.

- Individual loan payments per pay period must be limited to a level that would not cause financial hardship.

- Payday lenders are not to allow consumers to re-borrow immediately or carry more than one loan.

- Lenders can attempt to directly debit payments from borrowers' accounts a limited number of times if there are not sufficient funds to cover the loan payment.

Even with these protections, the federal government cannot regulate your behavior and habits. It's your responsibility to educate yourself on matters of personal finance, and reading this book is a great start. You can avoid using these establishments by exercising discipline in your saving and spending.

I am not a fan of borrowing money from family members or friends because these situations rarely leave relationships unscathed. However, if a payday loan is your only option, a friend or family member may be your better bet. The agreement of repayment terms should be in writing. This may seem a little extreme for people who love you. Don't take it personally. A family or friend loan should be treated as an official transaction so that everyone is aware of the terms and expectations for repayment. If everyone is committed to upholding their end of the agreement, the risk of ruined relationships is minimized.

Sam's situation highlights the necessity for establishing the ever-so-important emergency fund to cover the unexpected. Going forward, even though Sam is living paycheck to paycheck, he must make whatever sacrifices he can to build an emergency fund. This might include getting a side hustle.

MORTGAGE DEBT

Many personal finance experts consider mortgage debt acceptable because it's considered an investment. Real estate typically appreciates in value. As an investment, if you are a good steward of the property by taking great care of it, the future value of the property should be worth more than what you paid for it.

Although there are a growing number of individuals who are saving and paying cash when purchasing their homes, the reality is that most people are not in a financial position to do that and will need to finance their home purchase with a loan. When you secure a loan to purchase a home, you are mortgaging the house. As a security measure, the bank will hold the title (ownership document) until the loan is repaid satisfactorily. If you are unable to pay the loan as agreed, the bank (title holder) can take the house back. Your loan is considered a secured loan. It works the same way as a loan for a car. Technically you don't really own the home until you receive the title, but for all intent and purposes you are considered the homeowner, and you're entitled to the all the benefits and challenges that come with this great responsibility.

Another reason this type of debt is considered acceptable is that the lender can recover the property through a process called foreclosure, resale the home, and attempt to recoup any losses if the borrower does not pay as agreed. The idea is that the lender can be made whole. With unsecured loans like credit card and student loan debt, if you are not able to repay your loan, the lender has nothing to recoup and therefore cannot be made whole. People of good character do not purposefully forego paying what they owe. *"When you vow a vow to God, do not delay paying it, for he has no pleasure in fools. Pay what you vow. It is better that you should not vow than that you should vow and not pay."* [a] When you sign a loan document or promissory note, you are in fact promising the lender that you will repay the loan by the terms. You should be a person of your word and make every effort to clear your debt.

I was talking to a 25-year old young man who was in the process of buying a newly built home. During our conversation, he tried to convince me that buying a home was cheaper than renting. His rationale was that he was already paying $1,400 in rent, and his anticipated monthly mortgage alone would be $1,200. He mentioned that utilities (electric and water) were included with his rental. I told him that as a homeowner, he would now be responsible for all utilities, to include a quarterly water and sanitation bill, taxes, homeowners insurance, homeowner association fees and any home and yard maintenance and repairs. When he considered the additional expenses, his excitement waned. He'd already paid the required down payment with a credit card, and he signed on for a 30-year mortgage. To top it off, the bank approved him for a $220,000 loan on a $40,000 salary. This should be criminal.

"For which of you, desiring to build a tower, does not first sit down and count the cost, whether he has enough to complete it? Otherwise, when he has laid a foundation and is not able to finish, all who see it begin to mock him."[b] Contextually, this passage refers to the cost of discipleship or following Christ. But, the principle is that you should always take the time to research before making decisions. View your purchasing decision from all angles before committing to something that you may not be able to see to the end. If you purchase a home or any other big-ticket item with a long-term commitment and are not able to manage the payments, you subject yourself to public embarrassment. The bigger consequence is that you place yourself in a bad financial situation. I don't want to discourage you from home ownership, but you must be informed and prepared. I think everyone who desires to invest in a home should do so. Buying a home may likely be your biggest investment and material blessing. However, if you don't carefully plan such an important purchase, it may be your biggest financial nightmare.

Mortgage Interest Rates

There are two ways interest can be applied to mortgages. Payments may be structured using a fixed mortgage interest rate or an adjustable mortgage interest rate known as an ARM (Adjustable Rate Mortgage). Interest rates fluctuate based on the decision of the Federal Reserve--the agency responsible for adjusting interest rates to control inflation. If the economy is doing well, rates will likely increase. Conversely, rates decrease when things aren't looking so well. Lower interest rates encourage individuals to spend and borrow, which spurs the economy.

A fixed rate of interest is just that, fixed. It is the rate of interest you agree to pay on the principal balance, and it never changes. Some individuals will refinance the loan if they find a lower rate. This simply means they assume another loan to pay off the current loan, pay the new loan at the lower rate, and save money in interest.

An ARM starts out at an unbelievable low interest rate that results in a lower monthly mortgage payment. However, after three or five years, the interest rate is subject to change (usually an increase) each of the following years up to a maximum. So, while you have some comfort in knowing what you're paying for those first few years, there is no certainty on the amount your payment will change over the next several years.

For example, a typical ARM may start out with caps or terms like a 5/2/5. This means the loan has an initial cap of 5%, a second periodic cap of 2%, and a lifetime cap of 5%. If your interest rate is 4%, the initial cap or first adjustment is the 4% plus or minus the initial adjustment of 5%. This means your rate could rise as high as 9% or decrease to 1% with your first adjustment. The periodic cap dictates that subsequent adjustments will be capped at 2%. So, your rate can increase or decrease by 2% each year, but it cannot go any higher than 9% over the life of the loan.

What might an ARM look like for a $150,000 mortgage? For a 15-year mortgage, your monthly payments could be anywhere between $1,109 and $1,367, and payments would total $228,000, of which $78,000 is interest (assuming annual adjustment increases of no more than 2% with a cap of 9%).

If you compare the ARM to a fixed interest of 4% on a 15-year mortgage, your monthly payments would be $1,109 for the life of the loan. Your total payments would amount to $199,716, of which $49,716 is interest. You do the math. It seems to me that saving

$28,000 in interest payments and the security of knowing what you're paying each month makes more sense.

Some buyers assume ARMs with the idea they can refinance before the rate escalates. There is no guarantee that you'll be able to refinance later or what the state of the economy will be. This was the mindset of many individuals stuck in their ARMs during the 2008 economic crisis. They were unable to refinance because the value of their homes decreased significantly putting them in an upside-down situation; homeowners owed the bank more than their homes were worth. Because of the adjustments, the payments increased to the point where homeowners could no longer afford the monthly payments and the homes eventually went into foreclosure.

There may be some situations where an ARM may seem appropriate. If you know you're going to keep the house for a brief time during the initial term before the rate adjusts, an ARM might be a prudent idea. This is usually the case with military personnel who tend to relocate every few years. It doesn't eliminate the risk, but it reduces the chances of paying higher adjustment rates. Because of the uncertainties and contingencies surrounding an ARM, I do not recommend this type of financing for your home purchase.

Mortgage Loans

If you're thinking about purchasing a home, make sure you choose your mortgage wisely. Choosing a mortgage involves researching banks and credit unions (my financial institution of choice) and the interest rates charged for a 15-year fixed-rate mortgage. Research the type of loan that best fits your situation. Before choosing one of the three types of loans, consider factors such as, whether you have a down payment, your credit score, and your military status. The three basic loans types are Conventional, Federal Housing Administration (FHA), and Department of Veteran's Affairs (VA).[8]

Conventional loans are private loans and are not backed by the federal government. Since the lender is on the hook for any losses, the qualifying criteria for these loans are more stringent. Borrowers must have a minimum credit score, steady employment, evidence of a savings account, a down payment, and a low debt-to-income ratio (the percentage of your income dedicated to paying your current debt). Also, the down payment must be at least 20% to avoid having to pay private mortgage insurance (PMI), which protects the lender if you default on the loan.[9]

FHA loans are open to everyone and are guaranteed by the government. Because the government promises to cover the lender's loss, the requirements are less stringent. You can assume one of these loans with a down payment as low as 3.5 % of the purchase price. PMI is required but is not as high as the conventional loan. FHA loans are also more lenient with the debt to income ratio. There are loan limits, and fees are rolled into the loan. These loans are best for those who have limited savings and average credit scores. First-time homebuyer programs typically use FHA loans.

VA loans are also backed by the government but are offered only to qualified veterans and surviving spouses. There are no income restrictions and no down payment requirement. VA loans also do not require PMI. These loans benefit individuals who have lower incomes, no savings, and average or lower credit scores. Even though these loans do not require a down payment, I recommend that you be well on your way to establishing your fully funded emergency savings. You should be prepared for financial misfortunes before entering such a large debt commitment.

GUIDELINES FOR PURCHASING A HOME

If you've identified home ownership as one of your goals, you want to make sure that you're prepared. I recommend that you consider the following before signing on the dotted line:

Establish your emergency fund. An emergency fund should be established and consist of at least three to six months of your total expenses. These funds should be used only in the event of a true emergency like a job loss or other situation that causes a significant and sudden decrease in income. Your emergency fund gives you time to recover or make the necessary adjustments to accommodate the loss of income. If you lose your job or have an extended illness, it may take you months to recover. The last thing you want is a mortgage obligation while dealing with a financial emergency for which you have no money to resolve. Even if you purchase a new home, things happen that may not be covered by your homeowners insurance. Acts of nature can cause major damage, and you'll need to pay an insurance deductible before coverage kicks in. Things that you would normally call a landlord to fix, like a leaking faucet or a malfunctioning garbage disposal, will now be your responsibility. It's extremely important to have that emergency fund set aside before you purchase a home.

Clear all your debts. You should be debt free including student loan debt. Does this mean you must wait up to ten years to purchase a home because of your student loans? Not necessarily. Remember, it's all about your priorities and how you want to allocate your money to reach your goals. If you choose to pay your mortgage and student loans simultaneously, understand that your other financial goals, like savings, investments for college and retirement or that bucket list vacation may go on hold. Ideally, you want to be in a situation to where the only debt you have is your mortgage. Eliminating all other debt allows you to maximize contributions to other goals.

Save for a down payment. Most advisors use the rule of thumb of accumulating a down payment of 20% of the home purchase price. You can apply a smaller down payment. But, to avoid PMI and decrease market risks you'll want to maximize your down payment. One advantage of making a down payment is that it provides security when the housing market becomes unstable. To illustrate the impact of a 20% down payment:

If the housing market takes a turn for the worse as it did in 2008 and the value of homes plummet, a down payment provides greater protection against an upside-down mortgage. For example, let's say you want to purchase a home for $200,000 with 20% down. You'll have invested $40,000 into the home. If the market temporarily goes bad, your home that was once worth $200,000 is now worth $160,000. If you must sell the home, you will repay the bank their $160,000 and be clear of your debt because of your down payment. Had you not made a down payment and financed the entire $200,000, you would be upside down in that you would owe the bank $200,000, but you only have $160,000 from the sale of the house. You are still indebted to the bank for the remaining $40,000.

On the other hand, if the market does well and the value of your home increases to $240,000, you're at an advantage because of the equity you've built. Equity is the difference between the amount of money the home is worth and the balance owed, and it represents your share of the home's value. Because of your down payment, your equity in the home that you purchased for $200,000 with a $40,000 down payment is now $80,000. Of course, both examples assume that you've held the home for a brief period, but it helps to understand the concept and importance of having a decent down payment.

Another advantage of providing a sizeable down payment is that you may not be required to purchase private mortgage insurance or PMI. This is additional insurance besides your regular homeowners insurance. PMI protects the lender. If you default on the loan, the insurance company will pay the bank the money you owe. PMI can cost up to 2% of your loan balance each year. The first year of your $200,000 mortgage, a no-down-payment loan will cost you an additional $4,000 in PMI. Once you've paid 20% of your principal (the base part of your monthly mortgage payment that does not include your homeowners insurance, interest, or taxes), you can notify the lender in writing to discontinue the PMI premiums. At your closing (an event where the paperwork is signed to finalize the home purchase), you will be given a statement of how many years and months it will take you to reach that milestone. Think about this: With some loans, the 20% down payment is what lenders require to consider you trustworthy. The way I see it, you can practice delayed gratification and make temporary sacrifices to save the down payment and putting your money in an interest-bearing account until you're ready to buy. Or, you can finance the full mortgage (which means you're going to pay significantly more interest over the life of the loan), and pay PMI premiums until you reach that magic number. It makes more sense to save for the down payment, earning interest on the savings, and use it to build equity (ownership) in your home rather than paying thousands of dollars in premiums to an insurance company over several years with no tangible benefit to you.

Having a down payment also improves your chances of qualifying for your mortgage loan. Cash is always a good bargaining tool. The more money you have up front, the more comfortable the lender feels about loaning you money.

If you've already started saving for retirement by opening a Roth IRA (Individual Retirement Account), you should know that after five years you can withdraw money from that account with no penalties if the money is used for a down payment on a home. If you know that you'll be purchasing a home in five years, investing in a Roth IRA may be an option. Your contributions will earn much more in a Roth IRA than a traditional saving, money market, or certificate of deposit account. If you decide not to buy a home, you can continue contributing toward your retirement goals or your kid's college fund, which are the other two reasons funds can be withdrawn without penalty.

You should also consider federal programs that provide grants to encourage home ownership. There are grants that provide down payment assistance for first-time homebuyers. Many of you are not aware of these programs, or you don't apply for them because you assume you won't qualify. As an accounting manager for a local government entity, I've reviewed quite a number of these grant awards, and many of recipients are millennials. Some of the awards are as much as $25,000, and a substantial number of the homes are new construction. Programs differ from state to state so check with your state for specific program eligibility requirements.

For more information on home buying and home buying assistance in your state, visit the U.S. Department of Housing and Urban Development's (HUD) website, **www.hud.gov**.

Choose a 15-year, fixed-rate mortgage. It makes absolutely no sense to pay for a home for 30 years. I understand the argument that it gives you a tax break. This is nonsense because the interest you are paying over 30 years wipes out any tax break you're likely getting. For a $150,000 home at a 4.25% fixed interest rate on a 30-year loan, your monthly payments would be $738, and you end up paying a total of $265,648, of which $115,647 (44%) is interest. If you go with a 15-year mortgage at the rate of 3.625, your monthly payments would be $1,082, which is $344 more. But, the total payments amount to $194,680 of which $44,680 (23%) would be interest. That's a savings of $71,000! Besides that, you get to own and enjoy your home debt free 15 years earlier. The fun part is figuring out what to do with the extra $1,082 in your budget each month. If you're at the upper end of the millennial age, say 34, you could be mortgage free by the age of 50, which is still relatively young. Think of all the wonderful things you could do with those funds like building wealth. If you're already in a 30-year mortgage and you plan to remain in the home, consider making extra payments towards your principal This will shorten the number of years to pay the loan. For example, on that same 30-year mortgage, paying an extra $150 a month saves you over $36,000 in interest and your home will be paid off nine years sooner.

Limit monthly payments to 25-35% of your net income. Principal and insurance should be included in the monthly payment as part of the 25% to 35 % of your net income (take home pay). You must get your budget in order so you can determine how much of a monthly mortgage payment you can truly afford. Your home purchase should be based on what your budget will allow. Don't shop for your dream home and then try to force it to work in your budget. Some realtors will try to get you into a home that you love but cannot easily afford. It makes no sense to be in your dream home and not be able to buy furniture or pay the utilities. You don't want to be "house poor," meaning you have the dream home, but you are a prisoner to it because you can't afford to do anything else without going deeper into debt.

I was 31 years old when I purchased my first home. My husband at the time and I were being reassigned to Peterson Air Force Base in Colorado Springs, CO. We had no other debt. Having been pre-approved for our loan before arriving, we started house hunting immediately. We informed our realtor of the price we were willing to pay for our home. He began showing us homes selling for much more than we wanted to pay. After about three or four showings, I'd finally had enough and asked him why he was showing us these more expensive homes. He looked surprised and told us that our pre-qualification documents indicated that we were qualified for $100,000 more than the price we gave him. He assumed we were going to purchase a home for the maximum amount the lender was willing to loan to us. We had a budget, and *we* were telling our money where we wanted it to go. The lender and the realtor have their own interest in your home purchase. The more you spend on a home, the bigger commission the realtor gets and the more interest the lender makes. Don't allow them to tell you where your money should go. You are in charge. Long story short, we found a home that we loved and was priced within our budget. It was also much bigger than we anticipated. When we transferred four years later, we sold the home for $25,000 more than what we paid. Our frugality allowed us to freely enjoy our time in Colorado because our money was not tied up in enormous monthly mortgage payments.

GETTING OUT OF DEBT

If you're in debt, whether it be consumer, student, or mortgage loan debt, the first thing you should realize is that you are not alone. Millions of others are walking in your shoes. You do not have time to wallow in the guilt and shame of past behaviors. Forget about it. If you are willing to change your behavior, seek fulfillment in things other than material possessions, and become a better steward of the money God allows you to manage, you are heading in the right direction towards a life of purpose, joy, and abundance.

Before attempting any efforts to eliminate your debt, the first thing you should do is pray for God's guidance. *"Trust in the Lord with all your heart and do not lean on your own understanding. In all your ways acknowledge him, and he will make straight your paths."*[c] Changing patterns of behavior is not an easy thing, and you will need the guidance of the Holy Spirit to be completely successful. If you have the will, God has the way. Once you have sincerely communicated your desire to God and acknowledged that you need help, it is time to act. Below are some practical things you can do to eliminate debt:

Reduce expenses. More than likely, you're going to be making some lifestyle changes. You can start by making a list of the expenses that are essential, like rent and food, and eliminate things that are not essential like cable television. Do you really need 500 channels? The objective is to find money to pay off debt by reducing expenses. You may find that you can live without cable.

Increase your income. If you are not able to decrease your expenses, you must figure out a way to increase your income. I know you enjoy your free time and the thought of getting another job is nowhere near appealing. But, if you're serious about getting out of debt, you must do what you *have* to do now so that you can do what you *want* to do later. It's about sacrifice, and it's only for a season. What can you do to increase your income? Ask for a raise or apply for promotion. Sell your skills (writing, hairstyling, tutoring, typing, fixing cars or computers, etc.). If you work standard hours, perhaps you can get a part-time weekend or evening job.

Create a budget. Create a budget based on your actual monthly income and actual expenses—again, the bare minimum. You'll want to do a zero-based budget (see Chapter Nine). A zero-based budget requires every single dollar of income to be assigned to an expense or savings. Your budget will be an active reference tool. Once you create your budget, commit to following it. I cannot stress enough the importance of your budget in helping you manage debt.

The snowball payoff method. I first heard of this plan while listening to the Dave Ramsey radio show. With the snowball method, you'll list all your debt balances from smallest to largest, ignoring the applicable interest rates. Your focus is on the loan balances. This includes all debt (credit cards, car loan, student loans, and personal loans) except your mortgage. Once you have all your debt balances listed, you'll pay the minimum amount due on all the balances except the smallest. For the smallest balance, you will pay as much as your budget allows above the minimum payment. Once you get that balance paid off, you'll use the newly freed up money to add to the minimum payment of the next smallest balance. Repeat the process by working towards the largest balance until all debt is paid.

The avalanche payoff method. This method requires you to list all your debt balances from the debt with the highest interest rate to the one with the lowest. Like the snowball plan, you will pay the minimum payment on all other balances and apply all that you can to the balance with the highest interest rate. Work your way down to the balance with the lowest interest rate, and continue this pattern until your debt is eliminated. The snowball method focuses on the size of the debt balances, and the avalanche method focuses on the size of the interest rates.

Which of the two methods are better? It depends on what motivates you and how disciplined you are. Mathematically speaking, the avalanche plan will eliminate your debt faster and cost you less in interest. Although the avalanche method may get you there faster, some people tend to give up paying the loan with the highest interest rate. If you're working on a large balance, it may be discouraging trying to get that first win.

Millennials tend to be motivated by quick results and the feeling of having accomplished something. Using the snowball method, when the smallest balance is paid off, it's like a pat on the back and gives you a sense of accomplishment. It happens quickly enough that it motivates you to move on to the next challenge to experience that joy again. Even more motivating is when you see the progress you've made. It then becomes a game to see how quickly you can eliminate the next balance.

You can Google "Snowball vs. Avalanche calculator" to find a calculator where you can enter your debt balances and applicable interest rates. The calculators will give you the number of months for payoff and the total amount paid toward interest under both methods. Studentloanhero.com and magnifymoney.com are two sites with these calculators.

The three-year payoff plan. A third method is to total all your debts, excluding your home mortgage. Divide that amount by 36 months. This is the total amount you will allocate to your debt accounts each month. For example, using the three-year payoff plan, the allocations for multiple debt accounts are shown below:

Debt Account Name	Balance / 36 months	Monthly Payment
Student loan	$30,000/36	$833
Car	$9,000/36	$250
Credit card (total)	$7,000/36	$194
Total Monthly Debt Obligation	**$46,000/36**	**$1,277**

To pay off all your debt in three years, you would need to come up with $1,277 each month.

Loan consolidation. This method of reducing debt gets a bad rap, but there is a right way to use loan consolidation. If you have multiple debt accounts with varying interest rates and are overwhelmed trying to keep up with everything, consolidating your loans into one will make the payment process easier. However, the only time you should consider consolidating your loans is if you're going to end up paying a lower amount *overall* for the debt you're consolidating. This means you will not extend the terms (the length of time you must pay), you will not get a higher interest rate, and you will consider any fees associated with the consolidation. Even though the consolidation may yield smaller monthly payments, it may end up costing you more because of fees and interest paid over a longer period. Google "loan consolidation calculator" and select one of the results to locate a calculator. Input the requested information related to your loan terms to see if you're getting a better deal with the consolidation. You should note that combining your loans into one nice package is no benefit if you don't learn to change the behavior that created the debt in the first place. If you continue your same spending habits, you will end up right where you started.

Credit Card Balance Transfer. There are credit card issuers that offer 0% APR interests. The purpose is for you to transfer the balance of your high-interest credit cards. This saves you money by not having to pay the interest portion of your debt. Although this seems like a great deal, you must be very careful. The 0% interest rate is only good for a limited amount of time like six months or a year. At the end of the introductory period, the interest increases to a more traditional APR. The 0% interest may not apply to any additional charges made on the card. Also, there is a transfer fee of about 3% of the amount transferred. Google "credit card balance transfer calculator" to help you determine if a balance transfer is a good deal. Although this can be an effective way to reduce debt by eliminated interest payments, if your spending behavior doesn't change, you risk being in worse shape. Many individuals begin to charge on their old cards again. Or, they start racking up additional charges on the new credit card. If you don't intend to change your behavior, and only *you* know whether that is possible, I suggest staying away from this method of debt reduction.

***Contact your lende*r.** If you are having hardship and can't figure out how to pay your debts, contact your lender and explain your situation. They may be able to work out a new repayment plan, reduce your interest, or settle for less. If you are several months behind on your payments, a lender may settle for less than your balance owed. If you negotiate a settlement amount, once you pay that amount in full, the debt is removed. Make sure you get the settlement arrangement in writing. In any event, don't accept any offer where you end up paying more in the long run. If you don't feel comfortable or confident negotiating with your lenders, find a friend or personal finance coach who can assist you. Do not pay a debt consolidation company to make calls on your behalf. You shouldn't pay anyone to do what you can easily do yourself.

Maintain discipline. To get extreme results, you must do extreme things. Get rid of the credit cards. Cut them up today! Don't start hyperventilating. You *can* live without them. Exercising self-control will help you change your spending habits by changing your desires and priorities. It will be a struggle, but if you stay the course, God will lead you through the process. *"Commit your work to the Lord and your plans will be established."[d]* That is a promise from God. If you commit to the process and depend on Him for guidance, your plan to get out of debt will come to fruition. He cannot lie!

One of the challenges in getting out of debt is fighting through those periods when you might feel deprived and discouraged. You won't be able to do some of the things you see your friends doing, like going on vacation or buying new toys. You should learn to resist those feelings. You are on a mission. Explain to your friends that you won't be doing happy hour every Friday or that you won't be engaging in those weekly trips to the mall. If your friends have your best interest at heart, they will understand and help you achieve your goal by finding less costly alternatives for entertainment. If they are not supportive, you might want to provide some distance while working your plan.

Honor God with your financial giving. Determine a dollar amount (between you, the Lord, and your spouse) that you will give back to God on a regular basis and joyfully honor that commitment. *"...whoever sows sparingly will also reap sparingly, and whoever sows bountifully will also reap bountifully. Each one must give as he has decided in his heart, not reluctantly or under compulsion, for God loves a cheerful giver."*[e] Operating within God's plan, you can give and still come out ahead.

Seek wise, Godly counsel. No man is an island unto himself. A financial counselor or someone who has "been down that road" may be able to help you navigate through the task of eliminating debt. One of the best things you can do is find an accountability partner who will support and encourage you to stay on task. Even better, perhaps you can start a small group by enlisting individuals who are on the same mission. Your group should meet periodically to share accomplishments, struggles, and to provide support and encouragement.

Start today. No more excuses. It is time for you to free yourself. God does not want you in debt. There are better and more rewarding things to do with the money that has been entrusted to you. Dr. Tony Evans, pastor and founder of Oak Cliff Bible Fellowship in Dallas and chaplain of the Dallas Cowboys, posted on Facebook, "God can make the rest of your life be the best of your life. Trust him. He has a plan for you."

* * *

1. If homeownership is one of your financial goals, what steps are you taking to bring you closer to that goal?

_____

_____

_____

_____

_____

_____

2. If you have multiple accounts of debt, which method of debt elimination would you consider using; snowball, avalanche, or the three-year plan and why?

_____

_____

_____

_____

_____

_____

CHAPTER 6

Family Dollars

Do two walk together, unless they have agreed to meet?
(Amos 3:3)

One of the leading causes of deteriorating marriages is conflict over money. Couples enter marriage having different beliefs and attitudes about money that influences their behavior. When you have two individuals with different attitudes towards money and spending, disagreements will occur. How you manage those disagreements as a couple can make or break your relationship. Disagreements can provide opportunities to develop a more loving and trusting relationship as you communicate and work through the conflicts. Let's look at a few profiles of individuals from diverse backgrounds and the possible effects on relationships.

Sharon comes from a family environment where money behaviors were extremely conservative. There was a heavy emphasis on saving, investing, and spending for necessities first. Whenever Sharon wanted something that her parents deemed frivolous, she had to endure a lecture on the importance of saving and not wasting money. As a teenager, when Sharon got her first job, her parents forced her to save most of her paycheck.

Terrance comes from a family who struggled to make ends meet. His parents' income barely covered their needs. It was rare for Terrance to own things like video games or the latest athletic shoes. Terrance started working at the age of 16 and worked throughout high school and college. Thankfully, his family qualified for financial aid to cover the cost for Terrace to attend the local university.

Naomi's parents spared no expense when it came to providing for their princess. She wore the best designer clothes, took elaborate spring break vacations, and dined at the finest restaurants. Rarely did she hear the word "no" from her parents. Money was no object, so there were no limits to the amount she could spend. Naomi never held a job until she graduated from college and started working in the family-owned engineering business.

To some degree, these millennials' backgrounds may resemble yours. They represent the mix of people who enter relationships without having a full understanding of how different financial backgrounds can influence the dynamic of their relationships.

Sharon and Terrance's attitude may be shaped by their upbringing in two extreme directions. For example, Sharon may become a conservative money manager like her parents, or she may behave the opposite. She may enjoy the freedom to spend without the judgment of her parents. Now that she's calling her own shots she can spend money however she wants.

Terrance may experience insecurities about money that may cause him to be an ardent saver and a very frugal spender out of fear of not having enough money. On the other hand, he may become a big spender to make up for the times he felt deprived as a child. If Terrance enters a relationship with Naomi, who was raised to believe that there are no restrictions or limits on spending, the couple will have money problems. They may have difficulty agreeing on financial goals or how to manage the budget.

When couples argue over finances, often it's because they don't understand the reasons behind their spouse's behavior. Why does your spouse act like a tight wad? Or, why does your spouse continue to buy things the family can't afford? Taking the time to understand one another's behavior will make a difference in how the two of you communicate and approach solutions. If you agree on certain financial goals and one of you deviates from the plan, try to understand what's driving the behavior. However, one's upbringing should not be an excuse for repeatedly deviating from the financial plan. If you've addressed the issues and the negative behavior continues, it then becomes a matter of defiance, which is an even bigger problem.

The ideal time to discover if you are fiscally compatible with someone is *before* you commit to spending your lives together. Being aware of your own behavior and expectations in managing money is the place to start. If you know you're a tightwad or a frugal and conservative spender, you should be alarmed if the individual you're dating is a big spender, particularly if they're going into debt. You should date someone long enough to observe their spending and saving habits. Observe whether they set financial goals and work towards them. Are they high maintenance? Do they insist on brand-named everything? Do they appreciate gifts you give, or are they more focused on the monetary value of the gifts (materialistic)?

It's not enough to simply observe. During the dating process is when money conversations should take place. The first few dates may not be an appropriate time but certainly when the relationship is progressing and even more before an engagement. If you're seriously dating, chances are you're looking for your lifelong mate. You must have those hard conversations about money even if it makes you uncomfortable. Don't allow embarrassment or fear keep you from being proactive on something so critically important. Your financial future depends on whether the two of you are on the same page. Having the same attitudes about goal setting, spending, saving, giving, and investing, will make financial planning go smoothly. When you decide that the relationship is likely to be long term and possibly lead to marriage, there are four basic questions you should ask one another:[1]

1. What are your financial assets (savings, investments, and property)?

2. How much debt do you have (credit card, student, personal, and car loans)?

3. What is your income?

4. What is your credit score?

Having all financial information on the table gives you a starting point from which to base your goals. If you don't know what you're working with, you can't make smart decisions. If either of you owns a hefty amount of student loan debt, how are you going to handle that debt? Separately or together? Will you delay marriage until the debts are paid? Or, do you marry and consider all debt jointly and work on it together? If you're planning on buying a home right away, the credit scores will be a consideration. Do you need to clean up your credit to qualify for the best loan rates? And if so, do you work on your credit scores before or after marrying?

You will do well to decide how you're going to handle these situations before you marry. There should be no financial surprises after "I do." Respect one another enough to be completely open and honest about your financial situation so you can make informed financial decisions. What you think may be a deal breaker may simply be a matter of working through the situation as a couple. If your mate loves you unconditionally, a bad financial situation shouldn't run them off. They should be willing to find a way to help you work through it. The question is not *if* you can move forward in the relationship, but *how* to move forward.

When discussing finances, it would be a good idea to discuss prenuptial and nuptial expectations. Engagements and weddings have become such a huge deal that young adults are going into debt creating massive wedding productions. The cost of the entire process, starting with the engagement ring, can be very expensive.

When choosing a ring, remove all tradition from your minds. Guys, you should purchase a ring that is commensurate with your salary. Ideally, you'll want to pay cash for the ring so you may want to start saving early. If you know you want to be married someday but don't have any current prospects, I advise you to start saving for the ring in anticipation.

Ladies, lose the expectation of receiving a ring that is way out of your boyfriend's salary range. And don't pressure him by hinting at the size of the diamond you require or what it should cost. There used to be a time when guys would blindly shop for a ring and surprise his intended with a proposal. Now, ladies are dropping hints, leaving pictures of rings on the kitchen table, or enlisting their bestie to tell the boyfriend what kind of ring his girlfriend likes. I totally get it. You want to wear something that you're going to love. My main concern is that you don't expect him to go into debt. Consider your reasons for wanting a large, expensive diamond engagement ring and realize that the size or cost of the diamond is not equivalent to his love for you. Don't lose sight of the main thing.

I'm quite familiar with the term and duties of a wedding planner. Recently, I learned there's such a thing as a "proposal" planner. What? What happened to the days when the prospective groom enlisted his friends and family to pull off a surprise proposal? Now, a professional proposal planner is hired to create elaborate events, complete with professional photographers and live bands, to pop the question.

And then there's the wedding. Most couples are funding their wedding themselves. I'm happy about that because my daughter is due to marry soon. I remember a conversation she and I had soon after she graduated from college. I don't know why we were discussing weddings because she wasn't dating at the time. She asked me how big of a wedding she would be allowed. After I'd finished laughing, I told her, "Honey, you can have as big of a wedding as you can afford, and anything from me would be gravy." Her dad and I had budgeted for college, not a wedding. I can tell you this--even gravy can be expensive.

Seriously. The whole nuptial process is a very exciting time, and it's very easy to get caught up in the planning of your special day and lose sight of mounting expenses. I suggest you have an engagement period long enough to allow you to save enough money to cover your wedding expenses. I'm very impressed with the way Danielle and her fiancé Ryan planned to cash flow their wedding. They set a date, created a wedding budget, and decided how much money they would contribute monthly. Ryan even worked a second job to make sure they stayed on target. Your wedding is but one beautiful day. You're going to have a lifetime together with dreams and goals. Starting a marriage with a huge pile of wedding debt is not the way to go and puts you further away from your financial goals.

When preparing for marriage and combining your lives, you must also consider how you're going to maintain and distribute your finances to cover routine bills and other financial transactions. Will you combine all your resources into one joint checking and savings account? Will you each maintain your own accounts and open one joint account to which you both contribute to cover obligations and goals? How much will each person contribute to this shared account? I have seen it work both ways, but I've known it to work better when the accounts are combined.

Some millennials are not too fond of totally combining their money and find alternative methods of managing finances as a couple. Millennial couples' top reason for maintaining separate finances is to maintain independence. Other reasons include the ability to track what's in "your" account, being able to spend without consulting your spouse, and maintaining privacy on what you spend.[2]

One of the reason it's challenging for couples to treat their money as one is because of the emotional attachment. Money often represents one's security, power, and prestige. People falsely gauge their worth or value by the size of their bank account. The selfish nature, unwillingness to trust, and dogmatic drive to maintain independence cause couples to be reluctant in sharing control of their money.

In one scenario, a couple may maintain separate bank accounts. They agree that each of them is responsible for certain individual household expenses. One may be responsible for the utilities and groceries, and perhaps they split the rent or mortgage expense. This is the kind of arrangement one would see among roommates.

In another scenario, a couple may "compromise" and have three different accounts--his, hers, and ours. The "ours" account represents the joint account to which both persons have access. The couple may feel this arrangement allows them the independence and pseudo-unity they desire. They determine the total amount of monthly expenses and agree to contribute their individual income percentage of the total household income to their joint account. They agree that no one can touch the joint account for personal spending. I know several millennial couples who manage their finances in this manner. These couples miss opportunities to create unity and maximize their resources. There's also decreased transparency in the marriage.

It's more difficult to create unity and work on shared goals when the resources are separated. There must be a great level of trust that the other is contributing to the financial goals as agreed. There's also the temptation to cheat, not with another person, but with the finances. Financial infidelity happens when married couples are deceptive about their financial activities. Excessive spending and hiding it and not divulging how much money one makes are examples of financial infidelity. It's difficult to set financial goals when everyone is not aware of the resources. Separate accounts simply provide less transparency and increase the temptation to keep secrets.

If you're already married and still have your finances separated, you should communicate with your spouse and find out why. Is there a trust issue? If so, talk about it and most certainly pray about it. If your marriage is experiencing conflict, don't be afraid to seek counsel. Under the surface, the issues may not really be about money or spending, but more of trust, resentment, selfishness, stubbornness, or other things masking themselves as money issues.[5]

Remember Lauren and Chase from Chapter One? They decided to move in with Chase's mom to save money for a home. The good thing is that they shared the financial goal of purchasing a home. Unfortunately, they didn't follow a plan. Each of them maintained their own banking accounts and had no idea what the other was doing. They both contributed to the "house" account, but the amount and frequency of the contributions varied. It was no surprise that they were not able to meet their savings goal.

The goal Lauren and Chase set should have been stated to include a measurable amount. For example, a goal for the couple may have been stated, "We will save $20,000 over the next 12 months, and the plan to reach the goal is to save $1,667 each month." They should have been specific as to each of their expected contributions. Lastly, they should have come together regularly to discuss their progress.

Although Lauren and Chase made more than enough money to meet their goal, neither of them changed their spending habits. They maintained their same standard of living, which consisted of weekly mall trips, weekend excursions, and regularly eating out. They continued living separate lives in managing their money. There was very little to no communication. They argued over money and blamed the other for their financial woes, neither of them fulfilled their end of the deal, and they did not take personal responsibility for their actions. They became frustrated and felt the other couldn't be trusted. These kinds of repeated behaviors surrounding money can lead to resentment, loss of respect, repeated arguments, and loss of intimacy. Unfortunately, many couples in this situation will end up divorcing.

Bad behavior with money can certainly derail family plans. Working together for a common purpose is always beneficial. Below are some benefits to maintaining joint accounts:[3]

- Combining accounts encourages regular communication about finances. Frequent, open, and honest communication fosters trust and greater intimacy.

- Working from one account provides a built-in accountability partner on spending matters.

- Joint accounts foster unity in money matters. You are more likely to be committed to decisions that you make together.

- Shared funds provide a sense of working together to meet financial goals. Working as a team will yield greater success. *"Two are better than one, because they have a good return for their toil. For if they fall, one will lift up his fellow. But woe to him who is alone when he falls and has not another to lift him up!"*[a]

- Sharing funds helps to understand that all household income is "our" money.

There may be situations where having separate accounts makes sense. For example, if one of you is a liberal spender while the other is a consummate saver, this may be a dangerous combination for a joint account. There could also be addiction issues that may put the family finances at risk. If you must keep separate accounts for these or similar reasons, you should still strive to be on the same page by communicating frequently. Having separate accounts does not eliminate the need to be completely transparent and honest about your earnings and financial activities.

"Therefore a man shall leave his father and his mother and hold fast to his wife, and they shall become one flesh."[b] This is both literally and figuratively speaking. Once you're married, you should no longer be dependent upon or influenced by outside relationships. The two of you should be united in mind, body, and spirit. You should operate in oneness by the Spirit of God who will guide you in making the best financial decisions for your family. This requires total and complete trust in one another. If you trust each other, you'll be more willing to turn over "your" money for the greater good of the family. All money and possessions belong to you equally, and both of you are responsible for the proper stewardship of everything.

Another issue you might face as a couple is income inequality. Income inequality happens when one of you has a significantly higher income than the other. This situation does not typically cause too much friction when the husband is the main breadwinner. Traditionally and biblically, the husband usually assumes the role of the main provider, leader of the home, the final decision maker, and the one who is ultimately responsible and accountable for the household. Many men tend to gauge their manhood by their ability to provide and earn money.

Because these traditional behaviors still exist to an extent, most conflict happens when the wife is the main breadwinner. With more women than men graduating from college and starting their careers earlier, income inequality is becoming more common among couples. Some of the negative consequences of income inequality include guilt, resentment, power struggles, overspending, and lying about spending.[4] If couples don't learn how to maneuver around these issues, the prolonged behavior and stress will wreak havoc on their marriage.

For the spouse who has the higher income, there may be a tendency to hold that badge over the head of the other as a sign of superiority. Their superiority makes them feel like they are entitled to have the final word on financial decisions simply because they contribute the most money to the household. They may feel resentment if the lower earning spouse spends too much money on "non-essentials." But as the higher earner, it's okay for *them* to spend indiscriminately.

The spouse who makes less may feel guilty when buying things. They may even forego things they need because they aren't contributing as much. They may also feel resentful for having to ask permission to spend or feel as if they are at the mercy of their spouse. Further anxiety comes from feeling that access to "joint" money is restricted. Finally, the lower earner may hide their spending or lie about it to avoid conflict.

To avoid potential conflicts resulting from income inequality, the first thing you must do is become less selfish. When you decide to marry, it is no longer all about you and your needs. You don't belong to yourself, and your money doesn't belong to you. Part of loving someone is being more concerned about their needs than your own. *"Do nothing from selfish ambition or conceit, but in humility count others more significant than yourselves. [4] Let each of you look not only to his own interests, but also to the interests of others."*[c] Whatever the earnings situation, all income is shared income. Budgeting decisions should be made considering both of your needs and desires.

What happens when the two of you cannot agree on a financial decision, and the disagreement is causing animosity or friction? For example, let's say a family member calls asking to borrow money for the third time this year. One of you flat out says, "No," and the other wants to help—again. What do you do? Not all decisions can be settled with a coin toss.

In these rare occasions when you can't find your way out of the round-a-bout, the best solution is to follow the principles established by God. He created a structure and hierarchy to ensure that the family operates in a manner that brings blessings to the family and honor to God.

When you come to an impasse, the first thing you should do is pray about the decision. In this example, don't pray for the other person to change their mind. Pray for God's guidance that He would give you wisdom to look at the situation with discernment and compassion. It may be that God wants you to show compassion by giving the money to the relative. Or, maybe God *doesn't* want you to provide the money. The denial of the loan may be a message to the borrower that perhaps it's time for them to manage their money better.

If you've prayed over a financial decision, whether it be how much to budget in a particular area, how much to save, or what purchases to make, and you still cannot come to an agreement, someone must make the call. The spouse should fully support the decision and trust that it was made in the best interest of the family.

Millennial women are taught to be independent, strong, and assertive. You're told you can do anything a man can do. You're encouraged to stand up for your rights and not let anyone treat you inferior. I raised my daughter to believe the same. Because of the "I-am-woman-hear-me-roar" culture, the model for final decision making within the family may seem archaic, and you may be reluctant to try it. But, since your generation is all about thinking outside the box, I'm sure you're up for the challenge.

Let's look at this from a new perspective. Within any team, organization, or business, there is a designated leader. The leader usually has a vice or a director who supports the vision of the leader and is responsible for executing the plan. Although everyone on the team provides input, the final decision rests with the leader.

Who is the leader of your home? Don't think of the leader as being the authoritarian or the one who gets to make all the rules. Think of the leader as being the one designated by God to be ultimately responsible for the family's provision and protection. Consider the following scripture:

Wives, understand and support your husbands in ways that show your support for Christ. The husband provides leadership to his wife the way Christ does to his church, not by domineering but by cherishing. So just as the church submits to Christ as he exercises such leadership, wives should likewise submit to their husbands. Husbands, go all out in your love for your wives, exactly as Christ did for the church—a love marked by giving, not getting. Christ's love makes the church whole. His words evoke her beauty. Everything he does and says is designed to bring the best out of her. And that is how husbands ought to love their wives. They're really doing themselves a favor—since they're already "one" in marriage."[d]

It's important to emphasize that the husband's position has nothing to do with his income and everything to do with his position and obedience to God. Even if he makes less money than his wife, the husband is not released from his responsibility to protect and provide. Growing up in this culture, this can be a difficult concept for millennials to understand. If you're willing to try it God's way, I am confident your family will experience the blessings that come with yielding to His order for the family.

God has given the tremendous responsibility of leadership to the husband. When you and your spouse discuss finances, you should make every effort to agree. There should be some give and take. If you reach an impasse, it will benefit the relationship if the husband is allowed to function as God intended by making those final decisions on behalf of your family. The decision should be made with the thoughtful consideration and valuable input of his wife. God has equipped wives with intellect and special "helper' insight, also known as women's intuition. It would be wise for the husband to take advantage of these gifts.

There is a caveat to this model. If the husband has a history of being irresponsible, incompetent, or otherwise reckless with money and that behavior has, or has the potential, to cause harm or detriment to the family or family's finances, he should willingly delegate the financial decision making to his wife until his issues are addressed. This may require financial education or counseling. The wife should extend to him the same thoughtful consideration and opportunity to provide input before making decisions.

When it comes to the administration of your finances, like who balances the budget or pays the bills, these tasks should be performed by the person who has the best aptitude and attitude in performing these duties. Some people enjoy being in charge of the books and making sure everything is paid on time. Both of you should commit to attending the monthly family meetings to discuss the budget, monitor progress, and ensure that the family is on track to meeting goals.

Children are not exempt from participating in family finances and should be included in executing the financial plan of the household. Your kids will model your behavior and attitude. They should be taught that money is finite, and there are limits to what the family can spend. If they don't see you practicing discipline but instead irresponsibly buying anything you want, this behavior will become the norm for your kids as well. You can begin the process of forming their money attitude by teaching them to practice self-control and delayed gratification.

For starters, stop buying toys or candy each time they accompany you to the store. Allow there to be some visits where your child gets nothing. What you don't want is for the toy-per-trip to become an expectation. If they throw a fit at the store, so be it. If you don't buy the toy, they're going to hate you for about five seconds. They'll get over it and so will you. If you practice this exercise with consistency, they'll come to learn that it's okay if they don't get a toy. You're helping them understand that sometimes they'll have to wait to get what they want (delayed gratification) and that they shouldn't always have the expectation that they're getting a toy just because they're in the store (entitlement). Learning these lessons early in life will make it easier for your child to apply discipline and self-control as they grow older, and the financial implications become much greater.

Don't overspend when there's an opportunity to reward your child for positive behavior or an accomplishment. Positive reinforcements don't have to be costly and should incorporate the principle of frugality. For example, if Suzy has difficulty focusing at school and is being disruptive in class, perhaps as a reward for practicing self-control for an entire week, she gets to choose her favorite dessert or movie. Maybe she gets to choose the family's weekend outing. The idea is to correct unacceptable behavior. If the rewards are huge and expensive as a trip to Disney World for brushing her teeth, you may create a whole new set of behavior issues she can "correct" to earn big rewards.

If your family is cutting back on expenses, consider your kids' extra curricular activities. Is it necessary for them to participate in multiple costly activities? I'm reminded of a couple who is struggling financially. They have two small kids, one in the last year of daycare. This couple's children are involved in basketball, karate, dance, soccer, church youth activities, and scouting. Both parents work full-time. Imagine the combined cost of these activities. Cutting back on some of your activities will not only free up money in the budget but also simplify your busy lives and allow more time for resting and connecting with one another. I wholeheartedly believe children benefit from extracurricular activities, but there is such a thing as overdoing it, especially if you're having financial struggles and have no emergency fund.

As you raise financially responsible kids, understand that they don't have to own the "best" of everything. Whatever you can *afford* to buy them *is* the best for your family. Sadly, people often equate the cost of an item to the quality. Kids grow extremely fast, and it doesn't make economic sense to buy expensive designer clothing that they're going to wear only a few times. Little Johnnie could care less if his shirt has a polo man on it. He'd much prefer a Spiderman T-shirt and sneakers that light up. If *you're* the one wanting him to wear the Jordan's and the Polo shirt, ask yourself why.

Insisting on buying designer or brand-named clothing because *you* value these things teaches kids to be materialistic. I'm not advocating that you should never splurge on your children. However, if you are struggling to make ends meet or working on building financial wealth and meeting other goals, you should consider the impact that a $49, sized 2T Polo shirt will have on your budget. You can probably think of much better uses of $49.

Dare I mention the ever-popular character-themed toddler birthday celebrations? I've seen young parents, who were struggling financially, spend upwards of $1,000 funding a birthday party for a two-year-old. These parties included the biggest bounce house, a clown, food for kids and adults, rental of a facility, decorations, and other party amenities. I have nothing against parents wanting to celebrate their child's birthday in a big way if they can afford to do so. Most kids would be okay with a party on a much smaller scale, but some of you worry about making big impressions. The party is not about what your child wants but more about what would be impressive to the adult attendees. Sometimes the focus is on upping the ante on another parent who gave a great party last year or the great pics you can post on social media (comparative influences).

My advice is that you give your child the best party you can afford and include it in your budget. Check your motives before throwing a huge affair. Chances are your toddler won't remember the more expensive elaborate happenings of the event. Would a smaller guest list of your closest friends at home or a park be more in line with your budget? Playing games and serving hot dogs and hamburgers followed by cake and ice-cream can be a fun time. More importantly, consider the precedent you set if you're giving your kids Cirque du Soleil when they're turning two years old. What will their expectation be when they're turning 16 years old? Don't set them up for a lifestyle where they find contentment or joy with elaborate things or events only. Teach your kids the joy of simply being with people they care about and who care about them. Show them how to be happy whether they have a little or a lot. This shapes their attitude about money and materialism and starts them on the road to making wise financial decisions.

If you make frugality a way of life while your kids are young, you're helping the family now, and you're preparing your kids for life by teaching them to become wise money managers. *"Train up a child in the way he should go; even when he is old he will not depart from it."*[e] This scripture not only applies to spiritual training but financial training as well. Teaching kids the wisdom of managing money at the earliest age possible is one of the most valuable gifts you can give them.

* * *

1. At what point in the dating relationship should the conversation on personal finance (assets, debt, income, credit health) take place?

_____

_____

_____

_____

_____

2. What are your thoughts on the model for making financial decisions when a couple disagrees?

_____

_____

_____

_____

_____

CHAPTER 7

Plan Prerequisites-Foundational Concepts for Budgeting

Many are the plans in the mind of a man, but it is the purpose of the Lord that will stand. (Proverbs 19:21)

The heart of any endeavor is a good plan. The plan for ensuring you meet your financial obligations is called a budget. Your budget is designed to keep you on the right track as you move towards your destination—financial freedom. You decide the specific goals and timelines of your plan. You determine the priorities, and your behavior determines how quickly you arrive at your destination. You have total control of your plan.

Before you create your budget, it is important that you understand three foundational principles. They are foundational because every budget decision and every dollar assignment should be built upon these principles. If you make financial decisions considering the principles of stewardship, giving, and eternal perspective, you *will* be financially successful.

STEWARDSHIP

Because you were raised in a society that thrives on materialism, it's very easy to develop the mindset that the whole purpose of living is to make money to buy the things that bring you happiness. The more things you have and the bigger your things, the happier you are. And, the more money you get, the more you want. *"He who loves money will not be satisfied with money, nor he who loves wealth with his income; this also is vanity."*[a] There's always going to be the next best thing to buy. But, guess what? God created you and gave you the ability to create wealth so that you can be a blessing to others. The truth is, as stated by Rick Warren, author of *40 Days of Purpose*, "It's not about you!" Your money, abilities, time, and possessions don't belong to you. *You* don't even belong to you. I know you've been told how wonderful you are and that this is your life to live and your money to spend. Therein lies the problem.

"The earth is the Lord's and the fullness thereof, the world and those who dwell therein."[b] All that you have and everything in this world belongs to God. Your house, money, clothing, cars—everything belongs to God. Your job is to be a good steward over all that He's loaned to you. As God's manager (or steward), you have been given a great responsibility. He's trusting you to manage His things with great care. As a steward, your life and your finances take on an entirely new meaning. One of the reasons you may be experiencing financial hardship and other life challenges is because you have not managed your blessings, including your money, from a biblical perspective.

If you want to be a good steward, below are some things you should *not* do:[1]

- Use money to keep up with social appearances

- Use money to feel important (you're already important from God's perspective)

- Use money to "appear" righteousness (flaunting your giving)

- Spend money to indulge an obsession (shopping, gambling, gaming, excessive entertainment)

- Spend money to buy love and affection (people should love you for who you are, not for the material things you provide)

- Pursue wealth through get-rich-quick schemes (lottery, pyramid sales, risky investments)

- Neglect to give to those in need (charity, local church)

- Neglect to pay your debts

- Neglect to save for the future (college, retirement,)

- Borrow to purchase things that depreciate (vehicles)

- Borrow using credit cards (cars, clothing, food)

- Fail to take responsibility for personal finances

- Fail to establish and follow a budget/plan

- Fail to plan

Now that you know all the things that *shouldn't* be done as a good manager of God's assets, you're probably wondering what a good manager *should* do. First and foremost, you should acknowledge that everything belongs to God. Second, take care of what He's loaned to you the same way you would want someone to take care of your things. Make sure what was loaned to you is in the same or better shape than when you received it. For example, when I fly to Atlanta or Buffalo to visit relatives, I don't rent a car once I arrive. Instead, I'll borrow one from my relatives. To show my appreciation, I'll make sure the car is washed and filled with gas before leaving. Likewise, you show your appreciation for the things God has loaned you by taking care of them. Your home, car, or other possessions should not be found in disarray.

Third, increase the value of what has been entrusted to you. Matthew 25:14-30 tells the story of a master who was going on a long trip and asked his servants to manage his money while he was away. He gave five units to one servant, two units to another, and one unit to a third servant. The servants who received five and two units invested what they were given and doubled the master's money. The third servant did nothing with his one unit. When the master returned, he praised the servants that managed their units wisely. For the servant who did nothing, the master rebuked him for being lazy and making excuses. The master then gave the servant's one unit to the servant who had five, saying *"For to everyone who has will more be given, and he will have an abundance. But from the one who has not, even what he has will be taken away."*[c]

There are two principles to glean from this parable. The first principle is that you should spend your resources on things that appreciate. Just as the servants invested their money and yielded a good return for their master, you should invest your resources in things that will yield a return. For example, if you purchase a home and take good care of it, chances are the home will appreciate and yield a return on your investment. Likewise, investing in a retirement account, like a 401(k) or IRA, will likely ensure that you receive a return on your investment to help finance your retirement years.

The second principle is that it doesn't matter how much or how little you have. It's *how* you manage what you have that counts. The master gave each servant different amounts of money. Two of the servants doubled their money by making wise decisions. If you do the right things with your money, you will be given more. If you are a poor manager, your resources will be taken away. This can be seen in people who are consumed with debt, waste money on get-rich-quick schemes, and indulge in frivolous spending. Being a good steward is living your life and managing your resources of time, talent, and treasure (money) in ways that honor God.

GIVING

God's desire is that you prosper financially, not for your own enjoyment only, but to freely share what He's given you. When you share with others, people are drawn to Jesus because of your compassion and generosity. *"He who supplies seed to the sower and bread for food will supply and multiply your seed for sowing and increase the harvest of your righteousness. You will be enriched in every way to be generous in every way, which through us will produce thanksgiving to God. For the ministry of this service is not only supplying the needs of the saints, but is also overflowing in many thanksgivings to God. By their approval of this service, they will glorify God because of your submission that comes from your confession of the gospel of Christ, and the generosity of your contribution for them and for all others."* [d]

God's desire is that you give and as a result, he will provide you with more. Being generous glorifies God. Knowing this, it becomes more important to be good stewards over your finances. When you are consumed with debt and participate in foolish spending, you're not able to give generously to kingdom work, which entails giving and serving others. Thus, you're not receiving the full blessings of God.

How much should you give? *"The point is this: whoever sows sparingly will also reap sparingly and whosoever sows bountifully will also reap bountifully. Each one must give as he decided in his heart, not reluctantly or under compulsion, for God loves a cheerful giver."* [e] This Scripture identifies three principles of giving. When determining the amount to give, there are three questions to consider:

1. Are you giving of your own free will, or are you giving under compulsion? When you give, make sure you are doing so willingly and not out of guilt from overzealous solicitors communicating guilt-inducing lectures. You should be content with the amount you decide to give.

2. Are you stingy or generous? Your return will be in the same measure that you give. God gives you wealth so that you can be generous. If you are giving from a generous heart, blessings come back to you generously. His blessings can take many forms; financial, spiritual, physical, or mental.

3. Are you giving cheerfully? There should be joy and gratitude in your heart when you give. If you are giving reluctantly with a bad attitude, it's just as well that you don't give at all. Giving with a bad attitude makes your giving legalistic and obligatory, and God is not pleased with this type of giving.

Whether you follow Christian principles or not, giving should be a part of your life. No budget would be complete without a line item for giving. For those of you who may be struggling with debt and living paycheck to paycheck, it's understandable that giving may be the furthest thing from your mind. Others may be able to give but just never really thought about it in these terms.

While researching information for this book, I was happy to find that millennials are not the self-centered generation that many have come to believe. Numerous studies reveal that as a millennial, you generously give toward issues you're passionate about. According to the Washington Post, a Reason-Rupe poll showed that 84% of millennials gave to charity in 2014, and 70% of you spent at least an hour volunteering for causes you care deeply about.[2] Blackbaud's Next Generation of American Giving report cited that in 2014, millennials gave on average, $481 to charity. You give differently in ways that use your penchant for technology, competition, and social media. Remember the ALS bucket challenge that went viral on social media? This phenomenon raised $115 million dollars for the ALS Association. The article revealed that your giving spirit is not always monetary, which is understandable given your lower salaries and higher debt, but you give more of your time and skills than any other generation.

When I speak to young adults about personal finance, I emphasize giving because it's directly tied to blessings and personal financial health. Your purpose on earth is not to get wealthy for the sake of being wealthy. You were designed to help and serve others so they can experience God's love and grace and develop a desire to have a relationship with Him.

Even the secular world realizes the benefits of living generously. Warren Buffet, a professed agnostic and CEO of the investment company Berkshire Hathaway, is the 2nd wealthiest person in the world (Bill Gates is #1) with a net worth of $73 billion. He is known for his generosity and pledges to give 99% of his wealth to charity.

Mr. Buffet is quoted as saying, "If you're in the luckiest 1% of humanity, you owe it to the rest of humanity to think about the other 99%." The point here is that we all have a moral and spiritual responsibility to help the less fortunate. It doesn't matter where you are on the scale of wealth; there is always someone who has less.

God will use anyone, regardless of their faith, to bless others and show that His principles of giving are universal. If God can use non-believers to bless others with a portion of their wealth, how much more will He use those who believe? God prospers people when they give to others, and He wants to work through you. Your motivation for being wealthy should be driven by your desire to help others. The two scriptures below sum up the indisputable law of generosity:

2 Corinthians 9:6-11, "The point is this: whoever sows sparingly will also reap sparingly, and whoever sows bountifully will also reap bountifully. Each one must give as he has decided in his heart, not reluctantly or under compulsion, for God loves a cheerful giver. And God is able to make all grace abound to you, so that having all sufficiency in all things at all times, you may abound in every clever work. As it is written, He has distributed freely, he has given to the poor; his righteousness endures forever." He who supplies seed to the sower and bread for food will supply and multiply your seed for sowing and increase the harvest of your righteousness. You will be enriched in every way so that you can be generous on every occasion, and through us, your generosity will result in thanksgiving to God."

Luke 6:38, "Give, and it will be given to you. Good measure, pressed down, shaken together, running over, will be put into your lap. For with the measure you use it will be measured back to you."

There are three principles of generosity we can derive from the scriptures above:

1. Whatever you sow (give) is what you will reap (receive). If you sow sparingly, you will reap sparingly. If you sow compassion, kindness, time, or money, you will reap the same.

2. God loves a cheerful giver.

3. If you supply seed to others, God will increase your storehouse of seed so that you can continue to give. When you help others through giving, you receive more resources.

It's also important to know that you may reap your blessings in a different season. A farmer plants seeds in one season and enjoys the fruit in another. You may not see immediate results of sowing into the lives of others. Rest assured, God will provide your harvest in due season. His timing is not your timing, but he is always right on time!

For some, it doesn't seem logical that giving is the key to getting more. Logic tells you that four minus two equals two. From God's perspective, four minus two may equal three, or ten, or twenty. When you give, the value of what you receive may not always be measurable or tangible. For example, what value would you place on a settled spirit, peace of mind, security, joy, the satisfaction of helping others, increased abilities and opportunities, and good health?

How do you know if you're giving enough? When it comes to monetary giving, the Bible teaches that 10% is the standard by which we *begin* to measure our giving. It is called a tithe. In the Christian faith, a tithe represents 10% of one's income that is voluntarily given to the local church to help fund the church's expenses and kingdom building ministries. Some people question whether God really meant 10%, if the requirement is still relevant, and if it applies to your gross or net income. If you have participated in Baptist church services, chances are you've heard one or more of the following statements:

"You are robbing God when you don't pay your tithes and offerings."

"Tithing on the gross or net income depends on whether you want a gross or net blessing."

"When you don't tithe, you are sinning against God."

Sometimes these phrases are communicated in a condemning and judgmental manner and received in the same manner by individuals whose faith has not yet grown to the point where they can willingly and joyfully participate in giving at that level. When I was younger, chronologically and spiritually, I heard messages on giving that made me feel unjustifiably guilty because of the tone. I became defiant because I felt like I was being pressured by church leaders who were constantly "begging" for money. It wasn't until I grew in my faith and came under the leadership of a pastor whose messages focused on God's grace and mercy that I began to realize the enormous ways I was experiencing God's daily blessings. Gradually, I developed a deep sense of gratitude. Although no one can ever repay God for all He does, I count it a privilege to give to the ministry and to others, whether it's financial, serving in ministry, or spending time helping someone get their finances together.

I believe in giving 10% of income as both a biblical standard and a starting point for learning to give generously. I also believe you should be led by grace and faith-based giving.

It's interesting how 10% can be valued differently depending on the situation. As an illustration during one of my Sunday School lessons, I announced that the new shopping outlet was offering 10% off everything. The students barely acknowledge my statement. I picked up my newspaper as if I had misread something and said, "Oh, my bad, it actually says 40% off everything." Suddenly, there was an air of excitement and chatter. I asked why no one seemed interested in the 10% off sale, and the general response was, "Ten percent? That's nothing. That's not even worth the drive." I repeated the sentiment, "Yeah, you're probably right, 10% really isn't very much at all. I guess I can understand why God asks for only 10%." And a hush fell over the room.

The guidelines of giving are very simple: You should give generously, sacrificially, freely, and with a cheerful heart. Don't let 10% be your reason for shying away from the church. In many cases, it's not that you're selfish or stingy, but you may be in a real financial bind. Sitting in church listening to a fire and brimstone sermon concerning tithing and knowing that you don't have 10% of your income to give can be discouraging. If this is your situation, I'm telling you to stop focusing entirely on that number. Seriously. As you learn more about God's faithfulness, His commitment to you, and how He desires that you prosper, you will see things in a whole new light, and you'll be inspired and excited to become a generous giver despite your income level or financial situation. If it is your desire to give more money, more time, and more of your talents, you need only to express that to God and follow His lead. Focus on building your relationship with Him. Learn who He is and what He expects of you, and let your relationship with God and your personal convictions guide your giving.

Now, I will say this: You can't ask God for an increase in wealth or income if you're not doing your part. The best way to have more money is to control your debt and spending. In some cases, it's not that God hasn't been generous to you, it's that you haven't properly managed what He gave you. Now that you're acquiring more knowledge and wisdom, I know you'll get better at prioritizing your spending, saving, and giving.

If you're in a situation where you truly can't yet give financially, continue to give your time and your talents through service. There are many opportunities for you to serve within your community or church. I've read studies that show how millennials have shunned corporate worship. I get it. Some churches haven't quite figured out how to engage you in service. Even so, you should know that the church needs you more than ever. Local churches need your amazing ideas, your knowledge and skills in technology, and your energy.

And, the children need mentors. Instead of focusing on what you may not be getting, why not focus on what you could be giving? You can give your time to church ministries and various community projects. The point is, you are not on earth to live unto yourselves but to serve and give to others. In turn, God will make sure that all your needs are met.

ETERNAL PERSPECTIVE

Life is but a moment, and you have only a certain amount of time to fulfill your purpose. Author Beth Moore says, "Having an eternal perspective helps you cope with the ups and downs of life, knowing that it is all temporary. All that will matter in eternity is the glory that came to God as a result of my life. I will be most blessed when God is most glorified. If I'm more concerned about God's glory, then I'm less concerned about hoarding, giving my kids the best stuff, being comfortable, seeking a life of leisure, or keeping up with my neighbor."[3]

An eternal perspective helps you focus on things that matter. Your time, talents and resources are diverted to things that make a difference in the lives of others and things that are conducive to building God's kingdom and bringing glory to His name. *"Beloved, I wish above all things that thou mayest prosper and be in health, even as they should prosper."*[f] In his book entitled, *Living in Financial Victory*, Dr. Tony Evans notes that the apostle was not only praying for believers' material prosperity but also for their physical and spiritual prosperity because they are all interrelated. Dr. Evans writes that there are people who make a lot of money and neglect the spiritual component and purpose of wealth. Thus they often live with empty souls and broken lives. On the other hand, there are those who live with a poverty mentality and avoid gaining financial wealth thinking they are spiritual by living a minimalist life.[4] Increase in financial wealth not only blesses you materially but also provides an opportunity to contribute to the needs of others. There is nothing wrong with wanting wealth. I repeat—there is absolutely nothing wrong with having the desire to be wealthy by society's standards. God does not frown on acquiring wealth. However, you should carefully examine your motives.

What if you viewed wealth and abundance differently than the world? What if I told you that true wealth and abundance are not defined by material possessions, and that wealth and abundance are achieved by what is given away? You might ask how you can gain wealth by constantly giving resources away. Think about it this way: Let's say you've come into a great sum of money. You meet with a financial planner who convinces you to give her your money to purchase stock on your behalf. Haven't you just given your money away? "But wait a minute Merrie," you might say, "That's not giving it away, that's called investing? I gave it away because I expect to get a return on my investment. I gave a little, but I'm expecting to get a lot more than I gave." Exactly.

Whatever you "invest" into others, you will receive a guaranteed return on your investments. You may experience returns through God's favor shown to you through the kindness and generosity of others. And you will certainly receive the best return on your investment in your eternal life.

Managing your finances is not such a tremendous feat when you do so with an eternal perspective. Remember, your time here is but a vapor. Your time in heaven is forever. Increasing your income allows you to acquire material desires for your enjoyment. That's a good thing. However, the greater benefit of increased income and personal availability is that it allows you to store up treasures for yourself in heaven. With an eternal perspective, you're not obsessed with material things because you realize they are temporary pleasures meant to be enjoyed for a limited time here on earth.

If you think God wants you to live a life of minimalism and give *everything* away, that's not the case. God does not frown on wealth or material possessions. He simply has a prerequisite—that you live a life of obedience to His ways. Wealth can be a powerful testimony of God's grace, mercy, and favor when those who possess it humbly acknowledge the source. And just as there are prerequisites to experiencing wealth, there are warnings. You must not be greedy (Luke 12:15, Proverbs 15:27); you should not ask for things just to be asking or to fill lustful desires (James 4:3); and you should learn to be content with what you have. If you can't be happy with what you have, getting more won't make you happy (Hebrews 13:5, Ecclesiastes 5:10). Finally, do not develop a *love* for money. It is the *love* of money (or things) that causes people to do evil things (1 Timothy 6:10).

"Do not lay up for yourselves treasures on earth, where moth and rust destroy and where thieves break in and steal, but lay up for yourselves treasures in heaven, where neither moth nor rust destroys, but where thieves do not break in and steal. For where your treasure is, there your heart will be also."[g] When you live with an eternal perspective, you invest in heavenly treasures by spending, saving, and giving in a manner that has a positive impact on others and brings glory to God.

* * *

1. When have you ever received something and knew that it was the result of having sown into someone else's life?

_____

_____

_____

_____

_____

_____

2. What can you do to improve your stewardship over your money and material possessions?

_____

_____

_____

_____

_____

_____

CHAPTER 8

Budgeting: Line Item Wisdom, Part I

For which of you, desiring to build a tower, does not first sit down and count the cost, whether he has enough to complete it? (Luke 14:28)

Yes! Just what you were waiting for. I can feel the excitement. Seriously, budgets can be very exciting. It's all about perspective. Some of you may view budgets as a self-imposed restrictive tool to remind you of all the things you can't do. Want to go to the concert? Oops—not in the budget. What about buying that new handbag? Uh, no—not in the budget. Surely you can purchase that new car you've been eyeing for the past year. Think again. Who wants to live like that? Executing your plan does not mean you should give up things you want. You must simply plan for them. The tool you use to execute your plan is your budget. I use the terms budget and plan interchangeably throughout this and the next chapter.

"Know well the condition of your flocks, and give attention to your herds."[a] Back in the day, livestock was used in much the same way we use cash to purchase things. If the flocks were in poor condition, they would not be worth very much. Likewise, if

you don't take care of your "flock," it won't be worth much of anything. In other words, you've got to make sure your money is right. Your financial health determines whether you will be successful in meeting your everyday needs, as well as your future needs. Watching your flock is where your budget comes in. Once you identify what you want out of life, you should document how you're going to get there financially. Your budget is a roadmap for intentional spending, saving, and giving that will help you achieve your financial goals. If you have a reasonable plan and are willing to follow it, you'll freely enjoy everything in this big beautiful world that God created.

One of the most respected authors and speakers on personal finance is Suze Orman. She is super smart and on point when it comes to advising individuals on managing money, debt, investments, etc. She wrote a book called, *The Money Book for the Young, Fabulous, and Broke.*[1] It wasn't until I began writing this chapter and looking for resources that I noticed that Suze Orman's book has very little to say about budgets, and in fact, she implies that young people wouldn't be interested nor spend time working the budget process (paraphrased). I disagree.

Dave Ramsey, another personal finance guru I follow, is huge on budgeting. I listen to his radio broadcast on my way to work every morning. He has a segment called "Debt-Free Screams" where individuals are invited to tell their story of overcoming debt. At the end of their testimony, they count down from three and then yell, "I'm debt-free!" It's awesome. People come from all over the country to Dave's studio in Nashville, Tennessee to do their debt-free screams. Many of them are millennials. As Dave conducts the interviews, listeners learn that most of the debt cleared by millennials is student loan debt. Some of these millennials have tens of thousands of dollars in debt that they've paid off in minimal time. Dave always asks the guests what they did that was most important to their success. My guess would be that 90% or more of them attribute their success to living on a budget. I'm telling you, the budget really is the deal maker. You can check out those debt-free testimonies for yourself. Search "Dave Ramsey debt free screams" on YouTube. While executing your budget, I encourage you to frequently watch these videos for motivation and proof that fixing your financial picture is very doable.

If you are serious about managing your money, you can't afford to bypass creating a budget. Your budget puts you in control of your money. You tell your money what to do instead of your money telling you what you *can't* do. A budget also helps you prioritize your life. Two things determine a person's priorities—where they spend their time and where they spend their money. We should spend our time on things and people that matter the most to us. If you take inventory of where you spend your time, you may find that most of your time is not spent on the things that you claim are most important. The same goes for money. Once you go through the exercise of identifying where your money is going, you may find that you're spending money on things that are not truly high on your list of priorities as it relates to meeting your financial goals. Therefore, you'll need to make spending adjustments. Our friends Lara and Chase claimed their priority was to save for a down payment on a home, but their spending habits did not line up with their priority, and they failed to meet their goal.

Once you learn the art of delaying gratification and practicing self-control, and when you realize that operating outside of your plan puts you further from your goals, you won't view budgeting as the monstrous task it's made out to be.

I understand you have a very busy life and just the thought of taking the time to identify and categorize your expenses seem daunting. One of the things I love about millennials is that you're always thinking of more efficient ways to do things. Budgeting will be no different. The good news is there are several free apps available to assist you in creating and maintaining your budget. Whether you like to keep it simple or if you're into more complex applications, there is a money managing app that fits your style.

Two free popular apps are *Wally* and *Mint*. Wally provides a clear breakdown of your daily and monthly budget. It works like the popular dieting app, *Lose It*. When you enter the cost of your purchases (preferably as soon as they happen), the app provides you an instant status of what you've spent to date and shows how close you are to the spending goals you've identified. If you're a visual person, this app makes it easy to assess your status quickly. Mint is a similar app and can be linked to your bank account if you choose. Both apps require a little time and effort on the front end to enter your initial information. Once you've entered everything, you'll love how easy and convenient it is to track your money.

Another option (my personal preference) is the app, *EveryDollar*, a Dave Ramsey solution. (No, I don't get paid for endorsements.) Several of my clients use this budget app and absolutely love it. It's easy to use and gets the job done. Many people who call Dave's radio show mention using this app as part of their debt free plan. If you're like me, and you don't care for a whole lot of bells and whistles, complicated graphs, and confusing instructions, this may be the app for you. There is a paid version of the app with advanced features, but the basic free app is all you'll need. It can be used on your desktop or mobile device, so there's no excuse for not recording your transactions. If you're not into apps, an Excel spreadsheet will do just fine. There's a sample budget spreadsheet at the end of Chapter Nine.

The bottom line is you will never get ahead financially if your outflow exceeds your inflow. Creating and following a budget ensures that you stay on track. You earn a finite number of dollars, and you simply cannot spend more than you make without creating a negative financial situation for yourself. Stop thinking of budgeting as something that's bad, scary, or something that's going to be tedious, time-consuming, and suck the life right out of you. Anything you want to accomplish, you must put some measure of effort into the process to be successful. I challenge you to change your perspective and start thinking of budgeting as a tool and process to help you meet your goals as opposed to being yet another dreaded task to complete.

Hopefully, you've acknowledged and embraced information presented in Chapter Two that addresses the need for self-control. Following your budget will require you to exercise self-control. Stay focused on the mission and don't give up. I promise it will become easier over time, and once you see the results, you will kick yourself for not starting sooner. I firmly believe you can do this. This one valuable tool will help you get out of debt, stay out of debt, plan for future needs and wants, and serve as your personal roadmap to financial success.

FIVE STEPS TO CREATING YOUR BUDGET

1. Identify your goals: Identifying your goals is the first step in the budget process. Write your goals down and assign them a deadline. Refer to Chapter Two under "Procrastination" for tips on setting goals. Your goals may be to get rid of debt, purchase a car or home, plan a wedding, save for your child's education, or start a business. List those goals in priority order, assign deadlines, and allocate money accordingly. The shorter the goal's deadline, the more financial emphasis you should place on that goal. Your goals and their priority will determine how you distribute your income among the various categories or line items of your budget. The funding of your budget line items must line up with your goals.

You may get sidetracked when executing your plan. For example, you may have allocated a certain amount of money towards your savings for a new car. The concert of a lifetime is coming, and you spend the money allocated to your car to purchase concert tickets. Consequently, your budget takes a hit and you don't have the money for your car savings. A minor setback—maybe. Because you are changing some long-standing spending habits, you may have setbacks. You must regroup, remind yourself of your goals, and recommit to changing your behavior. Setbacks will happen. However, they cannot happen too often if you plan to be successful in this journey. Make your goals your reference point. If you get sidetracked, pull out your written goals and read them aloud to yourself. Ask yourself if what you are purchasing is getting you closer or further from your goals and if it's worth the sacrifice.

2. *Track and analyze your current spending:* If I were to ask you how much you spend each month on eating out, music downloads, coffee, or any of your frequent indulgences, chances are you would highly underestimate these expenses. When my son first entered the military, he was clueless as to how to manage his new stream of income. He consistently ran out of money before the next payday and had no idea where his money was going. Being the conscientious money manager mom that I am, I insisted on having access to his banking account. In reviewing his transactions, I saw where he'd been eating fast food for three meals each day. I printed out his statement and highlighted all the fast food transactions (the entire page turned yellow). I took a picture of the page and texted it to him. The visual alone was enough for him to get a handle on this problem. He didn't realize that he was spending upwards of $600 each month on fast food. I've since learned that when it comes to my own millennials, ignorance is bliss. I've removed my name from his bank account to protect my sanity.

My point is that you cannot set your budget properly without knowing where your money is going, and that requires you to track your spending. I suggest you perform this exercise for at least one month. You already know what's coming in, but now you need to know how it's going out. Earlier I mentioned the apps available to track your expenses as part of your ongoing budget process. For this exercise, I want you to use a small hand-sized notebook to log your purchases as you go about your day. Try to capture every dollar you spend, whether it's purchasing a pack of chewing gum or a refrigerator, paying a bill, or giving someone cash. No matter how small or insignificant an outflow of money might seem, capture it. At the end of the month, all purchases you tracked will be used to create and fund the initial line items of your budget.

3. Create your budget line items: After completing Step 2, you should have a pretty accurate picture of where your money is going. Did you know you were spending that much on coffee? No worries. You'll figure out exactly where you need to make spending adjustments. Using your list of expenses, you can begin placing them in the appropriate categories or line items of your budget. You will create a zero-based budget. Your total income will be allocated to all your budget line items so that your income netted with your expenses equal zero. That's the goal each month. Some typical budget line items are shown below:

Housing	Entertainment	Childcare
Food	Social/Professional Memberships	Debt
Transportation	Personal Grooming	Savings
Clothing	Medical/Dental	Gifting
Life Insurance	Investments/Retirement	Other

4. Record each expense: Once you've documented your expenses, you're now prepared to create your initial budget (see Chapter 9 for sample budget). I'm showing you the manual process just so that you get the idea. Using the free apps will make budgeting a piece of cake.

Each expense you tracked must fit into an appropriate category on your worksheet. Below is a shortened sample of your worksheet. Complete your worksheet to include all the expenses you tracked in Step 2.

Housing	1,250 (total of all spending on housing)
Food	400 (total of groceries and eating out)
Transportation	100 (total spent for gas, car payment, etc.)
Clothing	100
Life Insurance	65

5. *Monitor your progress frequently*: Updating your budget should be done at least monthly. You'll enter your actual expenses from the previous month. Note the line items where you may have exceeded your planned spending or where you came in under budget. These are your adjustment opportunities. For example, if you exceeded your spending on entertainment or dining out and find that you did not allocate enough for daycare because they raised the rates, you may decide to make up the daycare shortfall by decreasing the frequency of eating out. Once you've identified areas for adjustments, you'll enter your income and projected expenses for the upcoming month. You can always move money from one flexible line item to another flexible or fixed line item as needed, but your overall budget should never exceed your income. An even better aim, especially when you're tackling debt, is to come in under budget and use the excess to decrease your debt.

It may take you a few months to get your budget more exact. Be patient with yourself. If you become frustrated, focus on your goals and remind yourself that your efforts will pay off. Do not expect to get this right on the first or second try. You developed your spending pattern over a number of years, and it will take time to change your habits. Discuss any budget shortcomings or challenges with your spouse or accountability partner and together come up with a solution for a better outcome the following month.

This is something that you *can* do. I promise that if you remain committed to the process, you will begin to reap the benefits and come to embrace budgeting as a way of life.

The remainder of this chapter and Chapter Nine will provide information and advice for each line item of your budget to assist you in deciding your spending priorities and funding for your budget line items. The amount allocated to each line item should be based on your goals and priorities. Your priorities should be driven by the foundations discussed in Chapter Seven; stewardship, giving, and eternal perspective, as well as your personal values. If you are struggling to right some financial wrongs, you'll discover information to help you adjust and move forward. For those of you who have not yet made major financial decisions or are not struggling with finances, this information will help you avoid financial pitfalls.

I've also indicated whether a budget line item is a fixed or flexible expense. Fixed expenses are those that remain the same for a duration of time, typically at least a year. This includes line items like rent and mortgage. Flexible expenses are those that are optional like cable, or they can be expenses like groceries and utilities which fluctuate from month to month based on your consumption. The line items are standard. You may have expenses that are not listed, and you can certainly add them to your budget. Your budget is a living document. You can add or remove line items to fit your needs. Let's get started!

BUDGET LINE ITEMS

Housing (fixed): This is the monthly cost of your rent or mortgage and homeowner association (HOA) fees. A good rule of thumb is that housing is no more than 35% of your take home pay. If that seems a little low, it may explain why some of you find it difficult to live within your means. Living within your means requires that your current salary—take home pay, is enough to meet all your expenses. It's just that simple. Often, what happens is the home or apartment that you can truly afford does not meet your expectations. You may think it's too small, not in the right neighborhood, too old, or has other shortcomings. Instead of compromising for housing you can afford, you go for what you *want* even though the rent or mortgage is 50% of your take home pay.

Without considering other financial obligations, you convince yourself that you can make the numbers work. A few months after moving in, you realize that you can't afford to go out with your friends. You can't afford the newer car but finance it anyway. You can't afford to give to others or go shopping. And since you don't want to give up anything, you begin using your credit card. Before you know it, you've gotten yourself in a financial crisis because you refuse to live within your housing allowance. This scenario is very common among millennials. Think about this when you are re-setting your financial picture to coincide with your goals. It may require making the sacrifice of temporarily downsizing your housing until you meet other goals. If you're in a situation where your dream house or apartment is causing you to be house-poor, remember that you're the one in control. You decide whether to continue down that path or make a change. If downsizing is not an option, perhaps you can supplement your income or consider a roommate to split expenses until you're in a better financial position.

Housing (flexible): This line item should include your utilities, cable/Internet, and renters or homeowners insurance. Electric, gas, and water expenses can be controlled by behavior. Adjusting your thermostat a few degrees and practicing water saving techniques like not running water the entire time you're brushing your teeth and taking shorter showers will decrease expenses. The bigger your apartment or home, the more expensive your utility bills.

For your cable and Internet services, consider whether you really need these services and to what extent. Do you need the extreme super-duper package with 500 channels? Consider using digital television that requires a special antenna for a one-time cost of about $30 and provides over 100 digital channels in some geographical areas. Many of you are already using the Internet to watch your favorite shows through video on demand subscriptions, like Netflix, Hulu, or Amazon Prime. The monthly cost for these streaming services is a mere fraction of a cable bill and offer a variety of shows.

Homeowners and renters insurance is a necessity. If you have a mortgage, most lenders will require you to carry homeowners insurance to protect their interest in the property. Insurance covers your property if something happens, such as a fire or an act of nature. It also covers your personal assets within the home and protects you from liability if someone is injured on your property. The cost of homeowners insurance varies and depends on the size, location, and value of your home. Search the Internet for quotes.

Renters insurance protects your assets inside of your rented space. Many millennials mistakenly do not consider renter insurance a necessity and don't bother purchasing it. If your apartment is damaged by fire or another catastrophe, insurance will cover the value of your belongings. If your tub overflows and causes water damage to the property or your assets within the property, your renters insurance removes your liability and covers the damages. The owner of the property is not liable for your things so don't look for the landlord when the electricity goes out for hours and your groceries are spoiled. With renters insurance, you can file a claim for your food loss.

As with any insurance premiums, you can't view the payments as a real-time transaction. In other words, you don't immediately get something material for your premium payments. What you get is peace of mind. Insurance is assurance and keeps you from having unexpected large out of pocket expenses. Don't pass on this very affordable protection. With a cost of about $15 a month, it's much less expensive than having to replace your belongings.

Food (flexible): You have some control over your food expenses by your choices and habits. This line item includes all food consumption costs, whether you're eating out or purchasing food at the grocery store. That daily breakfast sandwich or coffee can throw your budget out of whack big time. If you spend $2 to $3 for a breakfast sandwich and $3 for coffee daily, that luxury will top you out at $132 a month. If you also buy lunch, be sure to include those costs. Be careful of "social" eating. Millennials like to travel in groups, and that includes eating together. Going to a restaurant with the crew may be fun and relaxing, but that daily burger or salad, plus tips, can be costly. If you're spending $8.00 for lunch each day for 21 or 22 days of the month, you can top out at $176.00. If we add your lunch to your breakfast cost, that's $308 a month. Even if we cut that expense in half (because you've got to eat *something*), $154 is a nice chunk of money to apply to debt or savings.

Don't feel pressured to participate in lunch outings. If you're working your plan and it requires you to cut back on expenses, decreasing this activity is an easy way to add money to your budget. Be honest when you're invited to lunch. There is absolutely no shame in letting folks know that you're on a mission and that you'll be brown bagging it for a while. If you're not comfortable with folks "knowing your business," just politely decline the invite. Trust me; someone will be happy to catch you up on the latest shenanigans.

For a quick, inexpensive breakfast, try blending a fruit/veggie smoothie, grab a breakfast bar, yogurt, or an apple and make your coffee at home. I must admit that I am a huge fan of Starbucks House Blend coffee. Here's what I discovered—they sell Starbucks at the grocery store. And the best part is that it tastes the same. For less than $7 bucks, I can enjoy my venti sized coffee for about 12 days at $.60 a cup. And check this out: Unless you're really hyped on the green and white Starbucks status cup, Walmart sells a sleek 24 oz., tin hot/cold cup made by Bubba. These are the best insulated cups ever, and they come in the coolest colors. You can sip your hot coffee for about six hours. I've turned several millennials on to these cups.

Another way to save money in this line item is to use coupons—not the way your grandmother uses them. You certainly don't want to waste time cutting, organizing, and monitoring expiration dates. There's an app for that. Actually, there are several free apps, like Coupon Sherpa, Favado, and SnipSnap. These apps organize and store your scanned coupons. They'll also alert you when the coupons are nearing expiration and when items on sale match your coupons. You can even share coupons with friends. When at the checkout line, simply show the coupons on your cell phone to the cashier.

Transportation (fixed): This line item is for your car payment. If you don't currently have a car payment, or when you finish paying off your car, make sure you plan the purchase of your next car by including a line item for a newer car. The best way to purchase a car is with cash. Save for the car you're eventually going to need, and buy it with cold hard cash. Most people use debt to buy their cars because they haven't learned the art of discipline or delayed gratification. You don't have to save for a $30,000 car. Save the amount you need for the car you can afford. A good $5,000 used car purchased using cash is better than going into debt for a new $30,000 car any time of the day. Especially when you consider that a $30,000 car financed at 4% APR for 60 months, with a monthly payment of $552, will actually cost you $33,150, the idea of a used car is more appealing. If you insist on using a loan to purchase a car, make sure the loan payments fit into your budget. This is an area where millennials tend to stretch the budget. Even though your car payment may be fixed, you can control the amount of the payment by choosing the right car based on your needs and budget.

When choosing a vehicle, make sure you first consider the impact on your budget. Will you be able to afford the monthly payments and still meet other financial goals and obligations? Secondly, consider functionality. Do you need a full-sized sports utility vehicle for a small family and city driving only? The last consideration should be aesthetics. I understand that looks are important and you want a car that fits your personality and style. However, it's not good wisdom to choose a car based primarily on looks. In other words, don't spend money to look affluent or project a certain image. Too many millennials are driving their potential mortgages or kids' college education. With the number of cars and styles to choose from, you should not have a problem finding a vehicle considering these three factors; 1) affordability, 2) functionality, and 3) style—in that order.

The best option is to purchase a used car. Understand that "used" doesn't mean that the car must be a junker. My advice is that you never buy a new car because the value of the car drops as much as 20% the minute you drive it off the lot. Let's say you take out a loan for $20,000 to purchase a new car. When you drive off the car lot, the car is now worth $15,000. If you were in a situation that required you to sell the car, you'd still be on the hook with the lender for the balance of the loan, not the value of the car. If you have a car accident and the car is totaled, the insurance company is going to cut you a check for the value of the car at the time of the accident regardless of the cost of the car.

Two benefits of purchasing a used car are they usually result in lower monthly payments, and someone else has eaten the depreciation. Purchasing a used car that's still under factory warranty is ideal. If you have your emergency fund, you should be able to cover anything minor that may not be under warranty. By paying cash, the best benefit is that you'll enjoy not being in car debt.

Leasing a car is never a good deal. The main selling points are that you're always driving a new car (fewer car problems) and the payments are lower. There are more cons than pros to leasing vehicles. If you lease, you'll be making monthly payments for an item that you will never own, you're never free of monthly car payments, and you're unable to free up funds to put towards another financial goal, such as purchasing a new car with cash. Leases also have mileage restrictions with high penalties should you exceed the allowable mileage. At the end of the lease, you must either purchase the leased car, start over with a new lease, or purchase a new car. You're constantly starting over and making a down payment each time. In many cases, the down payment is extremely high to compensate for the lower payments. Leasing is just a no-win situation.

Transportation (Flexible): This line item includes expenses related to keeping the car on the road, such as fuel, car insurance, and routine maintenance. Again, your behavior may have some bearing on the extent of these expenses. For example, if you have a luxury vehicle or a large vehicle, like a truck or SUV, your fuel costs and routine maintenance expenses will be higher. Many luxury cars require more expensive premium fuel. When choosing a vehicle, make sure you can afford all associated costs.

Car insurance expense is very flexible if you're willing to shop around. Although most companies provide the same types of coverage, premiums may vary significantly because each company has their own rating system to determine risk. Car insurance premiums may be based on risk factors, such as driver age, sex, make and model of your car, the car's color, your home address, where you keep the car (driveway or garage), most frequent driving route, previous claims, and your credit score. These combined factors determine how likely you are to be involved in an accident. The lower the risk, the lower your premiums. The type and amount of coverage also weigh into pricing. There are several types of optional and required coverages.

Most insurance agencies offer free quotes from their websites. Compare pricing and coverage options with at least three agencies, and make the best choice based on your needs and budget. If you already have coverage, it might be worth your time to compare your rate and coverage to what's being offered by other agencies. If you find significant savings, switch agencies and allocate the money saved to another budget line item.

Liability protection is required by all states and protects you from out-of-pocket expenses for lawsuits resulting from injury to third party people and property. It's called third party because it involves someone other than yourself (your insurance company is the first party, you are the second party). The two types of third party liability insurance include bodily injury and property damage. Bodily injury covers medical, lost wages, and pain and suffering expenses of the injured party. Property damage liability covers the cost of the third party's car or other property that was damaged because of an accident. The amount of liability insurance purchased should be at least two times the amount of all your assets. If someone attempts to sue, your liability insurance covers the cost of damages alleged by the third party.

If you're hurt in an accident, you are the third party to the other person's insurance. There's a chance that the individual at fault won't have insurance. For this reason, some people purchase additional coverage to make sure they are taken care of in the event they can't recover their losses from the other person. This coverage is known as Personal Injury Protection or PIP. It's also known as "no fault" coverage. Regardless of which party is at fault, the policy holder will be covered for 80% of medical, funeral, and lost wages. Unlike bodily injury, PIP covers you and anyone on your policy. It even covers you when you're driving someone else's car if you have permission to use it. Many states require PIP coverage.

First party insurance simply covers your vehicle and includes Comprehensive and Collision coverage. Comprehensive covers almost any loss other than a car accident. If a tree falls on your car, comprehensive coverage will make sure your vehicle is repaired. Collision is a no-fault coverage for damage to your vehicle because of a car accident. Regardless of who is at fault, your car will be covered for repair or replacement at the current value. If you have a loan on your vehicle, the lender will require you to purchase both Comprehensive and Collision to protect their interest. You should buy an amount equal to the value of the loan. Once the loan is paid off, the coverage becomes optional. Your deductible amount usually correlates to the cost of premiums. If your premiums are high, your deductible may be low and vice versa. Since accidents are unpredictable, you won't budget specifically for your deductible. The deductible would be paid from your emergency savings. For more information on other types of coverages, visit DMV.org.

Other transportation expenses are your car's registration and license renewal fees. Registration costs may vary by vehicle type and age. You'll also want to include any costs for tolls and public transportation.

Clothing (flexible): Shopping is one of America's favorite indulgences. Although millennials' income is significantly lower than boomers' income, millennial women spend 33% more on clothing, and millennial men spend 50% more.[2] The good news is that you pride yourselves on getting the best deals by comparative shopping, searching online for coupons, and using brand or store loyalty programs.

Before shopping, consider what you really need. If you need a white shirt or blouse, make it a point to look for your white shirt as the first order of business. When shopping at the mall or online, don't browse. Browsing will take you off task and entice you to spend impulsively. Ask yourself why you make certain clothing purchases and if emotions or other reasons are driving your spending. Getting to the bottom of why you buy clothing that you don't need will be a starting point for correcting your behavior and saving money.

If you shop as a hobby and it's negatively impacting your ability to meet other financial obligations, find an alternate activity that's just as satisfying but less expensive. Before my daughter left for college, our Saturday routine was to hit the malls. Sometimes I overspent, and other times I spent nothing more than the cost of lunch. We never missed a Black Friday sale, and we meticulously mapped our route to get the best deals. My hobby of shopping was an activity of bonding with my daughter. I enjoyed the routines we created visiting the stores we both enjoy (Francesca's) and the laughter and joy of just being in each other's company. I had an emotional connection with shopping. When my daughter left for college, my routine changed. My Saturday routine of going to the mall just didn't *feel* the same. Eventually, I forced myself to fill my Saturdays with a different activity. Visiting bookstores had become, and still is, my Saturday muse. I can tell you that giving up those Saturday mall trips have saved me a lot of money over the years. I purchase a book from time to time (okay, *all* the time), but the cost is nothing compared to the money I used to spend on clothing. Sometimes, just changing your routine, the places you frequent, or the people you keep company with may be all that's needed to get rid of bad spending habits.

Some of you shop excessively because you want to make a statement with your choice of clothing. You've come to enjoy the compliments and praise of others extolling your magnificent style. Don't let compliments and positive feedback drive you into financial distress. Understand that clothes do not make you a better person or increase your value in God's sight. If you want to be impressive, perhaps your focus should be on impressing the one who is concerned with the way you dress your heart and the beauty that lies within you. *"… For the Lord sees not as man sees: man, looks on the outward appearance, but the Lord looks on the heart."*[b]

Unfortunately, people make judgments about you based on your appearance. Don't allow other people's meaningless assessment of you cause you to place so much emphasis on your outward appearance that you spend money you don't have. The most impressive thing about you that people will notice is not what you wear, but how you act, how you treat others, and how you honor God. This is what looks beautiful and what makes the difference to those who matter. When you're budgeting, consider clothing a category you can control by simply adjusting your behavior. You should always want to look your best, but you don't have to bust your budget to do so.

Entertainment (flexible): What do you like to do for fun? Perhaps you enjoy going to the movies, concerts, Netflix marathons, reading, video games, shopping, or attending sporting events. Whatever expenses are associated with your favorite activities should be included in this category. Include newspaper and magazine subscriptions. There are many opportunities to cut back on expenses in this line item. If you go to the movies twice a month, cut back to once per month.

Travel is very popular with millennials. Many of you would rather travel and have experiences as opposed to acquiring material things. Again, you set the priorities for your life. Keep in mind that you still need to prepare for your future. Do you opt for the big travel excursions now? Or, do you settle for smaller vacations so that you can address debt or other financial obligations? Whatever your choice, if traveling is important to you, it should be included it in your budget, and you should fund it with cash. Plan your trips well in advance and shop for the best pricing. Groupon.com and BookVip.com offer great deals on travel. Since many of the deals have short expiration dates, you may want to continuously contribute to your travel line item so that when a great deal pops up, you're prepared to fund it with cash.

While going through the process of building your emergency fund and eliminating debt, don't give up all entertainment activities. Everyone needs an outlet and means of decompressing. Choose activities that are inexpensive, or participate in your favorite activities less frequently. Search online for free activities in your area. If none of the activities capture your immediate attention, be adventurous and choose an event that you've never done. You may discover an exciting new interest and meet new people. There's a world of opportunity and discovery when you go to unfamiliar places and do things that you wouldn't normally do.

Cell phone service is another flexible budgeting opportunity. With the number of providers and plans available, this expense can span from very little to extremely large depending on the services or features you select. It pays to shop around for phones, carriers, and service plans. The smart phone is a convenient necessity, and there are plenty to choose from. Think about the features you need and stick to the basics when you're trying to save money. Refrain from upgrading each time there's a new model released. An upgrade typically means an increase in your monthly bill. Research to determine if it's better, in the long run, to lease or buy a phone. Don't rely on the salesperson for this information; they are likely to give you the answer that works best for their profit line.

Memberships/Social and Professional (flexible): If you belong to any social, community, or professional groups, like fraternities or sororities, chances are there are expenses involved. These expenses should be funded through this line item. Include costs of dues or fees and clothing or uniforms. Travel expenses for conferences, registrations, and meetings on behalf of the organization should also be budgeted here.

Personal grooming (flexible): When budgeting, you want to make sure you include the cost of products used for personal grooming. This includes money spent on hair, manicures and pedicures, toiletries, makeup, etc. Millennials tend to be very image conscience. After all, you must be selfie ready at all times, right? Charles Stanley, the Senior Pastor of First Baptist Church in Atlanta, is known for saying, "Always look your best, do your best, and be your best." There are ways to minimize grooming costs and still present your best self. Consider store brand equivalents of your favorite products (don't roll your eyes). Compare the ingredients of the brand-named item and the store brand. If the first five ingredients listed on both brands are listed in the same order, the products are virtually the same, but you'll pay about 40% more for the brand-named items.

How are you doing so far? Hopefully, you're gaining insight into the making of your budget and discovering ways to minimize expenses. Let's continue with more budget line item discussions in the next chapter.

* * *

1. Do you currently have a budget/plan? Why or why not?

_____

_____

_____

_____

2. If you have a budget/plan, what do you find to be the most challenging aspect of managing a budget?

_____

_____

_____

_____

CHAPTER 9

Budgeting: Line Item Wisdom, Part II

Commit your work to the Lord, and your plans will be established. (Proverbs 16:3)

C ontinuing with the budget line item expenses, we'll finish up with discussions on health/medical and life insurance, childcare, gifting, debt, savings, and investments.

Health/Medical (flexible): The subject of healthcare insurance has been a hot button topic lately. Regardless of the government policies in place, the bottom line is that you need healthcare insurance. Yes. You're young, healthy and you may even be a gym rat. That's all well and good, but your body is like a machine. Although it may run like a charm, it needs regular maintenance for optimal performance. Sometimes your body breaks down and needs to be repaired. You should make it a point to visit the doctor at least annually. These wellness checkups will typically include a general gender specific examination and routine blood tests. Most serious illnesses are curable or manageable when detected early. The Bible emphasizes the importance of good health. *"Beloved, I pray that all may go well with you and that you may be in good health, as it goes well with your soul."[a]* Just like it's God's desire that you be spiritually and financially healthy, He is also concerned about your physical health. You can't walk in your purpose very well if you're ill.

Medical insurance protects you from having to pay large sums of money at once for unexpected, expensive treatments. Paying full price for a medical procedure can be a major roadblock in your financial plans. For example, the average cost to treat a broken arm that does not require surgery is $2,500. If surgery is required, the cost jumps to $16,000.[1] If you get appendicitis and need your appendix removed, the procedure may cost you up to $35,000 without health insurance.[2] It's not a matter of whether you need health insurance, but a matter of what type and the costs.

Your healthcare budget line item should include the cost of premiums paid for medical insurance, prescriptions, and any copays for doctor visits. The best way to save on medical expenses is to take care of yourself. Annual checkups, regular exercise, and healthy eating may prevent serious illnesses, such as high blood pressure, diabetes, or high cholesterol. These health conditions require routine maintenance and monitoring. You'll have more doctor visits, co-pays, and prescriptions. You may also have to take time from work, which may cost you additional money.

Unless you are independently wealthy, health insurance is a must. If your job offers healthcare benefits, you should enroll in the employer sponsored healthcare plan. These plans are usually the most affordable. If you're enrolled in college, you may be eligible to participate in the college plan. If you're under 26 years old, you may be eligible for coverage under a parent's plan. Otherwise, you'll have to sign up through the Affordable Care Act's (ACA) open market. Before selecting a healthcare plan, you should be familiar with basic terminology:

Premium: The amount you are charged to participate in the plan. Your employer usually deducts premiums from your paycheck.

Co Pay: The amount of money you pay when you visit the doctor's office.

Coinsurance: A percentage of your medical costs for which you are responsible until your annual deductible is met. For example, if you have a plan that has an 80/20 coinsurance, the plan will pick up 80%, and you'll pay the remaining 20% of the cost of services.

Deductible: The amount of money you must pay out of pocket each year before your plan starts to pay.

Network: A group of medical providers under one umbrella. The plan you select may restrict you to doctors under that umbrella only.

Primary Care Physician: The doctor you routinely visit and is your first point of contact for health issues.

Referral: Authorization from your primary care physician that allows you to be seen by a specialist, such as a dermatologist, cardiologist, or an orthopedic. Some plans do not require referrals.

There are four different types of healthcare plans:

1. ***Exclusive Provider Organization (EPO)***: With this plan, you must visit a doctor, specialist, or hospital that is part of a pre-selected group of providers. This is a low premium/high deductible plan that pays, on average, 60% of medical costs. An EPO may fit your needs and budget if you don't expect to go to the doctor very much and don't take regular prescriptions.

2. ***Health Maintenance Organization (HMO)****:* This plan uses doctors who have contracted with the HMO to provide services at agreed upon prices. They cannot charge more for a procedure or treatment than the contract allows. The plan does not allow you to use a doctor who is not contracted with the HMO. You will also need a referral from your primary care physician to see a specialist. On average, these plans cover 70% of medical costs.

3. ***Point of Service (POS)****:* Premiums are higher, but you pay less for visits and medicines if you use the doctors and other healthcare providers in their network or group. If you require a specialist, you'll need a referral from your primary care physician. On average, this plan pays 80% of medical costs. If you visit the doctor often or require a lot of prescription drugs, this may be the plan for you.

4. ***Preferred Provider Organization (PPO)***: Like a POS plan, you'll pay higher premiums with a PPO. However, you'll pay less for doctor visits and medicines when using doctors or other healthcare providers in their network. If you're willing to pay a higher cost for visits, you can also use providers that are not in

the network, and you won't need a referral to see a specialist. This plan is usually the most expensive.

Before choosing a plan, study your options, compare all costs (premiums, prescriptions, copays/coinsurance, and deductibles) and select the one that best fits your needs and your budget. Don't forget dental care plans. In addition to the various healthcare plans, there are two programs with tax benefits that you may want to use in conjunction with your healthcare plan.

Flexible Spending Account (FSA): If your employer offers FSAs, they will advance you a dollar amount that you've determined is sufficient to cover your out-of-pocket healthcare expenses for the upcoming year. The money goes into an account that you access using a debit card to pay for things like deductibles, copayments, prescriptions, medical equipment, over-the-counter medicines, and eyeglasses. Your employer deducts the amount from your pay over the course of the year. The advantage of using an FSA is that you get the money up front and the amount deducted from your pay is pre-tax money. The potential downside is that you must have a fairly good idea of the amount you're likely to spend during the year. Any portion not spent is lost. FSAs are not available to you if you are insured on the marketplace under the ACA.

Health Savings Account (HSA): An HSA is like an FSA in that the contributions are also pretax. However, unlike an FSA, there is no use or lose stipulation. An HSA is essentially a personal savings account with a financial institution like your bank or credit union. If your employer does not offer HSAs, you can participate in the ACA marketplace. An HSA works like a 401(k) in that the funds continue to grow tax free. There are limits to the amount you can contribute. If you withdraw the money to pay for medical expenses only, there is no tax. Check with your employer or bank for other restrictions and rules for both the HSA and FSA.

Gym Memberships: Expenses for gym memberships should be included in your budget under healthcare because exercise is essential to maintaining good health. Gyms are quite popular among millennials. When choosing a gym, select one that fits your budget. Be careful of getting caught up in the grandeur and amenities of a facility. Your membership fees will include the cost of those extras. Select a gym that offers workouts conducive to your abilities and has the right atmosphere for you. Otherwise, you may waste your money. I learned the hard way the importance of selecting the right workout environment.

I once attended a bridal show with my daughter who had recently become engaged. One of the vendors was giving away trial classes to his boxing gym. I decided to sign up because I don't pass up too many freebies. The following Saturday morning, I went to my free introductory class. The instructor was extremely welcoming, and I was excited that I was the only one in the class. The instructor coached me through the entire boxing routine, and I had a fun time. So, what did I do? I signed up on the spot with an annual contract and purchased all my equipment—gloves, tape, etc., that same day.

The following Monday, I attended my first "real" class, and the gym was packed. Nearly every punching bag in this 4,000-sq. ft. facility was claimed. I was surrounded by millennials of all shapes and sizes. The music was blasting an unrecognizable hip hop beat, and I could not hear a word of the song over the bass. I looked around at everyone stretching and conversing with one another. The volume of the music didn't seem to be an issue. I thought, "Do these people not hear this music?" I tried to act like I knew the drill. I began stretching my legs and arms while trying my best to look cool and collected. Suddenly, the thunderous voice of the instructor burst through the speaker causing me to darn near jump out of my skin! He seemed to be announcing his name and credentials. I started thinking of ways to escape without being noticed.

To my surprise, I hung in there for the entire session and worked at about 70% of the intensity of the class. After four weeks of consistent attendance, I decided to give it up because the workouts were extremely intense, and my non-millennial knees were not cooperating. But, I remembered that I'd signed a one-year contract—I can't quit! There's no way I was going to lose $720. I'd crawl to the punching bag if I had to.

After speaking with the manager and explaining my knee situation, he reviewed my contract and pointed out the allowance for a 90-day exit. The exit stipulations were that I had to keep my membership for at least 90 days, and I must have participated in at least two sessions per week. What? I'd met the weekly participation criteria, but it had not yet been 90 days. Long story short, the manager sensed my desperation and showed mercy by allowing me to cancel my contract and receive a refund. Thank goodness! The lesson to you is this: Do not sign an annual contract. Gyms rarely refund membership dues. As for me, I'm back to video workouts and my elliptical machine that costs me nothing.

If you join a gym, make sure it's a pay as you go or month-to-month contract. If you purchase an annual contract, you'll put yourself at risk for losing your money. Life happens. Your situation may change to where using the gym is no longer feasible. You don't want to be stuck in a contract having to pay a full year's membership for something you can't use. If you can afford to join a mega-gym and you enjoy the benefits, knock yourself out. If you can't afford the higher profile gyms, stay away. I know it's very "in" to dress out in workout gear for which you paid top dollar to look good while working out. I get that. But again, if this whole gym thing is setting you back financially, it's time to do something different to achieve your workout goals. Consider joining a less expensive gym. Alternatively, there are plenty of free online videos on YouTube for any type of workout you desire. If you have space in your home, invest in workout equipment. Make sure it's truly an investment and not just another place to hang your clothes. You can buy equipment for less than the cost of some annual gym memberships.

Life Insurance (fixed): Life insurance is an extremely important line item to budget. A policy is purchased by paying monthly premiums. In return, the agency pays your designated beneficiaries a lump sum upon your death. Young people rarely think about life insurance because they don't typically think about dying. If you are young and have no one else depending on you for financial support, you don't need life insurance. However, regardless of your age, if you have a family or others who depend on your financial support, you need life insurance.

Life insurance is not for your benefit. The purpose of life insurance is to ensure that your loved ones continue to have financial support after you're gone. Purchasing a policy is one of the most loving and selfless things you can do. Losing a loved one is an emotionally devastating experience. The last thing your dependent survivors need is to be stressed and left wondering how their financial needs are going to be met. Life insurance allows them to continue living a lifestyle that resembles the one you planned together.

The amount of life insurance purchased should cover your burial expenses, any remaining debt—to include your home mortgage, your children's college education, and any other major financial obligations. If your spouse doesn't work outside the home or is a stay at home parent who may need to return to the workforce, you should also include daycare expenses. Consult with a financial planner to determine the type and amount of insurance to purchase. When speaking with a financial planner, keep in mind that they are in the sales business. Do your research before your meeting so that you have an idea of what you need and what it should cost. For example, you do not need to buy a life insurance policy for your children unless you are financially dependent on them, which is typically not the case. Be suspicious of any planner who tries to convince you that you need to buy a life insurance policy to cover your children. Some planners will offer products that have a college savings or investment feature tied to the policy; don't buy it. There are better ways to save or invest with much better yields.

There are two basic types of life insurance policies--term and permanent. Term policies provide protection for a certain period, such as 10, 20, or 30 years. In some cases, the premium stays the same for the duration of the policy. Read the fine print on your policy or ask the agent about rising premiums. Premiums for term insurance are very cheap, and the policy can be renewed at the end of the term. Upon renewal, the premiums may increase because they may be based on your age and health at the time of renewal. Certain health conditions make it more difficult to buy life insurance. If you're in poor health, you may be denied coverage, or your premiums may be extremely high. Remember, it pays to exercise and practice healthy eating habits because it saves you money.

Permanent life insurance policies include Universal and Whole life. These cash value policies are designed so that a portion of your premiums are deposited into a savings or investment account. Be aware that the return on these investments can be as low as 2%, and the premiums are significantly higher. Universal policies will typically allow you to change your level of coverage. Whole life policy premiums are fixed for the life of the policy.

I recommend low-cost term insurance. It doesn't seem wise to throw excess money into an investment deal with such low returns when you can apply that money to your 401(k) or Roth IRA and yield much higher returns. While you are young and healthy, purchase an affordable 30-year term policy. If you're the average millennial age of 26 and commit to living as debt free as possible, any debt accumulated, including your mortgage, should be paid off within 30 years. You'd still be relatively young and healthy (hopefully) and shouldn't have any problems renewing for a smaller amount of coverage for end-of-life expenses.

Childcare (fixed): The most important aspect of securing childcare is ensuring that your children are in a safe environment and receiving great care. Do your research to find the best care you can afford. Make sure your budget includes all costs associated with daycare, such as extended care, field trips, or other activities that may not be included in the regular fee. Consider alternative care costs for times when the daycare facility may be closed.

Gifting (flexible): I mentioned the blessing of being a giver as it relates to charity, supporting your community, and giving to your local church. Gifts to individuals should be allocated to this line item.

If you are known to be a giving person, this line item will likely present a challenge. The line item for gifting is rarely underspent, which can be a good thing because it shows one's generosity. However, in some cases, even generosity has its limits and gifting should be built into the budget. Millennials seem always to have an occasion to celebrate, and many of those unique events involve gift giving. From birthdays to one-year dating anniversaries, baby and wedding showers, and job promotions, you're always game for a celebration. And let's not forget gift-giving holidays, such as Christmas, Hanukkah, Valentine's Day, Mother's Day, and Father's Day. That's a lot of gifting.

At this stage in your lives, your circle of associates and friends may be steadily increasing as you meet more people and form new relationships. It's very easy for your gift list to become extensive, and it can be a challenge to adequately fund this line item with consistency. Unless you set gifting limits, for the number of people, occasions, and pricing, this line item becomes a moving target. As a flexible line item, adjustments can be made. You may have to eliminate individuals from your standard gift-giving list, and you should learn to be okay with that.

One of the challenges of gifting is reciprocation; do you, or don't you? Have you ever had a situation when you received an unexpected gift from someone for your birthday or Christmas? If so, what was your initial response? There was probably a look of surprise followed by expressions of gratitude, panic, and guilt. You may have felt bad or embarrassed that the person was not on your gift list. What did you do? You may have rushed to reciprocate or made a mental note to add that person to your list. This is one way your gift list continues to grow. Can I let you in on a secret? Most people who buy gifts for you do so from a genuine heart and don't expect anything in return. It could be that you've made an impression on them, offered a word of encouragement, or you were there for them when they were going through a rough time. A gift may be given for no other reason than to show appreciation. You must learn to respond with a gracious, "Thank you" when gifted unexpectedly and leave it at that. Just as you learn to give freely and gracefully, you must learn to accept freely and gracefully with no guilt aftertaste. Gifting should never be driven by guilt or obligation but from a genuine heart of joy with no expectation of reciprocation. You should also avoid "one up" and "match" gifting where gifting is turned into a competition from year to year. Purpose in your heart what you're giving and the amount you're spending and stick to it. It doesn't matter if your gift is not reciprocated or if the gift you receive is more expensive than the gift you gave.

If you have unlimited financial resources, you can give until your heart is content. Otherwise, you must set limits, not only on the dollar amount of the gifts but on the number of people you routinely gift. When budgeting, consider people you routinely gift. Create a list of those individuals and assign each of them a dollar limit that you can afford to spend. If you can't imagine crossing anyone off your list, you must adjust the amount allocated to each person. The total amount should be included in this budget line item.

If you're creative, check out Pinterest for inexpensive seasonal crafting ideas. Nothing says love like a personal handmade gift. Creating a special gift for someone means you've given them a one-of-a-kind gift, purchased with something far more precious than money—your time. Most people who are not driven by materialism love heart-made gifts. If you're a great baker or cook, bake their favorite cookies or invite your friends to your home for a home-cooked holiday meal as your gift. A Google search for inexpensive gift ideas will give you many gift options to consider.

Debt (fixed): This line item should include all debt--student loan, credit card, car, payday loan, personal loans, etc. If you have a mortgage, include those payments in your housing budget. When you create your line items for debt, you can lump all debt into one line item, or you may elect to create a separate line item for each debt for better tracking. Refer to Chapter Four for detailed information concerning debt.

Savings (flexible): This is one of the most important line items in your budget. Your ability and willingness to save determines when you'll meet your financial goals. One of the top complaints I hear from millennials is that you can't afford to save. The truth is you can't afford NOT to save. Whatever your salary, you should make your best effort to consistently save some portion of it each time you're paid. Recognize that some of the choices you make, such as living in too much house, acquiring debt, and consistently spending without a plan or purpose, undermine your efforts to save and ultimately defer your dreams. The first step in saving is to create insurance against the inevitable by establishing your emergency fund.

Emergency Fund Savings *(fixed):* Before tackling debt or saving for any other purpose, you should establish your emergency fund. Most personal finance experts recommend an initial fund of $1,000. The most common emergencies do not normally set you back any more than $1,000. This fund ensures you're prepared to deal with the unexpected, such as car repairs, bereavement related expenses, medical mishaps, and home repairs. Knowing you're covered for emergencies reduces stress and panic attacks when the car breaks down. It also prevents you from going further into debt by avoiding charges to credit cards, payday loans, or borrowing from your family and friends. None of these options should be your plan for handling financial emergencies. You can quickly establish your emergency fund by using your tax refund, selling items you're no longer using, and saving any work bonuses or raises.

The number one rule of an emergency fund is that it should never be used unless you have a true emergency. Finding a great deal on a fantastic getaway, buying that Black Friday electronic, or buying new clothing for special events are not emergencies. Also, someone else's emergency does not necessarily have to be yours. You should not use your emergency fund to support someone's bad habit or habitually poor choices. That's not to say that you shouldn't help those with authentic needs.

If someone asks you to loan them money, you have every right to ask the purpose so that you can determine if the situation constitutes an emergency by your standards. You should also take the time to pray for guidance. The Holy Spirit will let you know what to do. There are times when I've been led to say, "No" even when I wanted to help. I would later find that the individual resolved their situation on their own. Sometimes, God works through your "no" to teach someone a lesson. Other times, God may be teaching you about sacrifice and generosity. *"Give to the one who begs from you, and do not refuse the one who would borrow from you."*[b] God is not going to tell you to make a sacrifice if He hasn't already made provisions for you.

Once you've built your initial emergency fund of $1,000, you're going to forget about it until you have an emergency. If you must use any portion of the fund, your first priority in your budgeting process is to bring this fund back up to $1,000. Ultimately, your fully funded emergency savings should consist of three to six months of basic living expenses. This ensures you can still meet your basic needs if you should lose a significant amount of your income. A job loss or extended illness that renders you unable to work will be less impactful with a fully funded emergency savings account. However, don't start building this fund until you have paid off your debts (except your mortgage). Paying off your debts will allow you to build the full emergency fund more quickly because you'll have more money to contribute. For now, just focus on maintaining your initial emergency fund of $1,000.

Goal Savings (flexible): Once you pay off your debts and have your emergency savings fully funded, your focus should turn to saving for other financial goals. Prioritize your goals and then fund them as your savings allow. Try to save at least 10% of your income. You may want to save for several goals at one time. For example, you may want to buy furniture, make repairs or upgrades to your home, or fund that long-awaited vacation. Your time table and the amount of your savings allocated to each goal will be based on your priorities. If you decide that you *really* need a vacation to celebrate becoming debt free, then direct your savings towards your vacation. Commit to saving for your furniture and home repairs immediately upon returning from vacation.

Long term goals are things you want to accomplish five or more years from now and may include things like funding college for your kids, starting a business, saving for the down payment on a home, or saving for retirement. Long term goals are easy to identify but more challenging to accomplish because they seem so far off—out of sight, out of mind. Working toward long-term goals requires patience, consistency, and self-control over a longer period. When you're working towards long term goals, there's a tendency to become discouraged. At times, you may feel as if you're not getting anywhere, and things come up that tempt you to become distracted. *"And let us not grow weary of doing good, for in due season we'll reap, if we do not give up."*[c] Perseverance is the key. You'll reap the benefits in due time. Start saving for these goals as soon as possible to take advantage of compounding interest. Detours will happen and when they do, make sure you do what's necessary to get back on the right track. Your diligence will pay off.

The bottom line with saving money is that you must do it, and you must be consistent. Saving is the only way you're going to accumulate money to do the things you love doing or buy things you need or want without going into debt.

Investments/College Fund & Retirement (flexible)

For your long-term goals like college and retirement, the best way to fund both is to save through investing. These two major events will be staring you in the face before you know it. The question is will you be ready? As a millennial, you have the absolute best tool available to assist you in preparing for these future milestones. You have time. The earlier you start investing, the more prepared you'll be.

If you ask most millennials who are struggling with student loan debt what they would have done differently, you'll likely hear that they would have gone to a less expensive school, or they would not have assumed so much student loan debt. You should have a plan to make sure your kids get through college debt-free. You certainly don't want them to start their young adult lives with a mountain of debt.

If you ask most baby boomers who are retired or nearly retired what they wish they'd done differently to prepare for retirement, most of them will tell you they regret not having started saving or investing sooner. If you choose to continue working in your senior years, hopefully, it's because you *want* to and not because you *have* to.

While millennials are struggling to pay their student loans, retirees are still working to supplement their meager retirement incomes. If you don't want your children saddled with loans, and if you want to be able to enjoy your retirement years, you had better start a savings and investment plan as soon as possible.

Saving for College: The cost of college is rising exponentially, and federal programs that provide financial assistance are slowly being chipped away. In fact, the recently proposed federal budget calls for eliminating subsidized student loans; the government will no longer pay the loan interest while students are in college. The budget also proposes to end the student debt forgiveness programs for those who go into public service or teach in under achieving schools. Lastly, the proposal eliminates half of the funding for work study programs. What does this mean? It means that you should be prepared to fund college for yourself or your children by footing 100% of the bill. Student loans turned out to be less than the ideal way to fund college, and if the proposed budget passes, they will be an even worse alternative.

Each state sponsors 529 plans to encourage savings for college expenses. 529 plans are tax advantaged qualified tuition plans. With the 529 savings plan, you contribute money to an investment account. You can contribute as much as you want, and if the funds are used for your child's education, you can withdraw them tax free. The rules for the 529 plans may vary in each state. The beauty of the plan is that you can invest in any state, and your child can attend college in a completely different state. Since the plan invests in mutual funds, returns are dependent on the performance of the stock market. Over the long term, these funds have performed well yielding upwards of 8% return on investments.

Under a prepaid plan, you purchase college credits and room and board (dormitory) at today's prices. The price you pay is locked in, so you're protected from price increases. You can purchase the plan in one lump sum or make installment payments. Unlike the 529 savings plan, states require the plan to be used in the state where it was purchased (with some exceptions). Not all states have prepaid plans. Some states have both the 529 savings and prepaid plans. Make sure you do your research before committing to either plan.

Another method of saving for college is a Roth IRA. The investments usually yield much higher returns than a traditional savings account. Although these accounts are designed to be retirement savings, the funds can be withdrawn after five years for qualifying education expenses. There are no penalties and any money earned on your investment will not be taxed. If your child doesn't go to college, you can use the money for your retirement.

Investing for Retirement: When it comes to saving for retirement, you can't start soon enough. Unfortunately, very few companies offer guaranteed retirement benefits in the form of pensions. Additionally, funding for the Social Security program, a federal program that provides benefits to retired people, is constantly being threatened. My suggestion is that you plan for the worst-case scenario by taking your financial fate into your own hands to ensure you'll have the quality of life you desire when you retire. This means you must save and invest as if it all depends on you alone. The Bible offers several principles on the merits of investing and planning for the future. Proverbs 6:6-8 tells about the wisdom of the ant in that even without a ruler to instruct her, she prepares her food in the summer so that she'll have something to eat in the winter. Genesis 41:25-57 tells the story of how Joseph used wisdom in planning for the promised year of famine. For seven years, he instructed that 20% of each year's grain harvest be stored. When the year of the famine came, the people of Egypt had enough grain. In Exodus 16, God provided a daily ration of manna (food) for the Israelites as they wandered in the desert. He instructed them not to gather any more than they could eat for the day, except on the sixth day, they could gather enough for two days. Those who were remiss in gathering their extra portions on the sixth day went hungry. These stories illustrate that God clearly intends for you to plan for your future.

There are several options for retirement savings or investments. You could open a savings account, money market account, or place your money on certificates of deposit. These options are good, but they're not the better options. With these options, you're loaning your money to the banks. Banks invest your money in stocks and bonds earning approximately 8% to 12 % interest and then turn around and give you less than 2% interest at best.

I recommend you invest in stocks and bonds as part of a group known as mutual funds. Your contributions will be spread among multiple stocks and bonds. By doing so, your risk of loss is greatly decreased. The average return on mutual funds is between 10 and 12 percent—much better than 2% or less on a regular savings account. One way you can invest in mutual funds is through your employer's deferred compensation program by opening a 401(k), 457, or 403B account. These programs allow you to defer the taxes on your contributions and you pay a lower amount of payroll taxes. You will not pay taxes on your contributions until you retire and withdraw them. The premise is that you will be in a lower tax bracket at that time and pay fewer taxes on your total contributions. Many companies offer a deferred compensation match up to a certain percentage. My employer matches my contributions at 1% of my salary. To get this free money, I must contribute at least 1% of my salary. I suggest you start contributing at least the minimum required to get the employer match. Once your debt is paid off, you should increase your contributions until you are investing at least 15% of your income towards your retirement.

Consider these scenarios: If your deferred compensation account balance is $32,000 today and you continue contributing $300 each month for 30 years, with an annual return of 10%, you will have accumulated $1,209,733.28. If you start with a balance of zero today and start contributing $300 per month with a 10% return rate for 30 years, you will have $651,396.31. Early investing makes an enormous difference. It is totally possible for you to become a millionaire by the age of 56 (considering the average millennial age of 26); that is the power of discipline and compounding interest.

The other recommendation for investing in your retirement is the Roth IRA. We discussed the Roth IRA as an option for funding education and the down payment for a home. If your company doesn't offer an investment retirement plan, you can open your own account through a financial planner or a banking institution. I opened my account online through my credit union. Contributions to your Roth IRA will be from money that has already been taxed, so you'll pay no taxes when you withdraw the funds. Also, any money earned on the accounts are not taxed. The annual contribution limits are smaller than that of a traditional IRA.

You should speak with a certified financial planner to determine which investment options are best for you. Again, keep in mind that financial planners are in the market to make money. Do your research and don't allow yourself to be sold a bunch of financial products you don't need. When calculating returns, be sure to consider additional fees that may be associated with managing the funds. The important thing to know about mutual funds is that you must be in it for the long haul. Since they are investments in stocks and bonds, you should not freak out when the market fluctuates, and your account balance decreases. Long term investments require patience, and you must ride out the lows as well as the highs. The purpose of these accounts is to encourage people to save for retirement. Therefore, if you pull the funds out before the required age, you will incur a huge penalty in addition to taxes. The money can be withdrawn early without penalties under very restrictive conditions. For more information on IRAs and other retirement investment options, visit **www.irs.gov** and search for retirement plans or consult with a certified financial planner.

To carve out money for savings and investments, you may have to make sacrifices in other areas of your budget. For example, the money you're now saving on coffee by making your own can be used to save for retirement. More than 45% of young millennials (ages 18-23) and 35% of older Millennials (ages 24-35) have spent more money on coffee than investing in their retirement.[3] For you, it may not be coffee but some other frequent indulgence. There is good news for millennials who have secured full-time employment. Transamerica Center for Retirement Studies reported the following:[4]

- 70% of millennials who started contributing to their 401(k) did so at the age of 22.

- 71 % of millennials who were offered a 401(k) accepted.

- Millennials are contributing an average of 8% of their salary and 10% with the company match.

- Millennials have an average of $32,000 in their 401(k) accounts.

After you've paid off your debts, figure out how much you can afford to enter on your budget line item for retirement savings. While some of you would rather have your coffee, many of you have come to understand the importance of getting an early start on saving and investing. Manage your money as if you have a future.

* * *

1. Which budget line item would be the most challenging for you to manage?

_____

_____

_____

_____

_____

2. What actions should you be taking now to prepare for your retirement years?

_____

_____

_____

_____

_____

SAMPLE BUDGET

The Jones' Zero Based Budget		June 2017	
INCOME	**Budget**	**Actual Income**	
Kevin-Salary	2,100.00	2,000.00	
Sharena-Salary	2,200.00	2,200.00	
Kevin-Uber	300.00	300.00	
Total Budgeted Income:	4,600.00		4,600.00
FIXED		**Actual Spent**	
Giving	460.00	0.00	460.00
Saving	300.00	0.00	300.00
Retirement	150.00	0.00	150.00
Home Mortgage (incl Ins & tax)	875.00	0.00	875.00
Cell/Home Phone	160.00	0.00	160.00
Electricity	60.00	0.00	55.00
Debts			
Credit Card Payment 1 (Balance = $4,000, 16%)	200.00	0.00	200.00
Credit Card Payment 2 (Balance = $1,000, 9%)	250.00	0.00	250.00
Department Store Card (Balance = 18,000, 3.5%)	200.00	0.00	200.00
Student Loans (Balance = 18,000, 3.5%)	600.00	0.00	600.00
Car Payments (Balance = $5,000)	620.00	0.00	620.00
Total Set Expenses:	3,875.00		3,870.00
Flexible			
Books/Magazines	25.00	0.00	40.00
Groceries	400.00	0.00	440.00
Child Care	0.00	0.00	0.00
Clothing	300.00	0.00	300.00
Other	0.00	0.00	0.00
Total Adjustable Expenses:	725.00		780.00
Total Budgeted Income	4,600.00	Actual Monthly Income	4,600.00
minus	-	minus	-
Total Budgeted Expenses	4,600.00	Actual Monthly Expenses	4,650.00
Total Budgeted Balance	**0.00**	Actual Monthly Balance	(50.00)
Total Budgeted Balance must equal "zero"			

Budgeting Notes

1. In a zero-based budget, every dollar of income must be allocated so that the net of income and expenses is equal to zero.

2. If you're over or under budget on any line item, you can adjust your actuals for the following month. Remember, it will take a

few months to get the budget semi-perfected. As a living document, it will constantly change based on your financial circumstances and goals.

3. If you have expenses that are paid on a cycle other than monthly, calculate the annual cost of the expense and allocate 1/12th of the amount to each month's budget.

4. Before you begin using an app, draft your budget on a spreadsheet. This will enable you to enter your data quickly.

If you prefer to use a spreadsheet for budgeting, you can download a pre-formatted spreadsheet at **zerobasedbudgethq.com**.[5] Edit the fields to personalize the spreadsheet by including your budget line items.

CHAPTER 10

The Point of it All

The end of the matter; all has been heard. Fear God and keep his commandments, for this is the whole duty of man. (Ecclesiastes 12:1)

As an accounting manager, my job is to manage people and processes to ensure that my team fulfills its purpose. Our purpose is to safeguard taxpayer money by auditing payment requests for compliance with laws, processing invoices, and generating accurate and timely payments to suppliers. That's it. Sometimes, I must perform research to determine if an expenditure is allowable. Researching issues slows the payment process, but it is necessary. Staying focused on our purpose ensures our success, and any processes and practices that do not align with our purpose are discarded.

By the same token, you will only be successful in personal money matters when you recognize and operate within your purpose. Anything that hinders your purpose should be discarded. Some of the steps you'll take to manage your money will be a little time consuming, but they are necessary as part of your purpose. Everything I've discussed in *Money Management Wisdom for Millennials* can be summarized in ten statements. Each statement begins with an action verb, which means you must *do* something.

To be financially healthy and walk in your purpose free of stress, you must do the following:

1. Spend less than you make. You will never get ahead if your outflows exceed your inflows.

2. Avoid debt. Debt decreases your opportunities to save and prepare for future financial goals.

3. Eliminate impulsive spending by exercising self-control.

4. Maintain an emergency fund to avoid going into debt when the unexpected happens.

5. Avoid using credit cards. They are not free money, and you will pay to play.

6. Save for major future life events (college, retirement).

7. Give cheerfully and graciously with confidence that God will meet your needs.

8. Think eternally. Understand that there is more to life than right now. Spend wisely and invest your time, talent, and treasure in others for a much greater future return.

9. Live on a budget. Spend, save, and give *intentionally*.

10. Overcome your lack of self-control, procrastination, and the influence of others.

So, what is the point of it all? How you manage your money significantly impacts your ability to live out your purpose fully.

Poor money management may also limit the extent to which God wishes to bless you.

God has given you special talents that are to be used as part of your life's purpose. You may be talented at coaching, teaching, cooking, organizing, administration, etc. Whatever talent you have, use it in a manner that allows others to see and experience the love and character of God through you.

If you have the gift of teaching, it doesn't mean that you must preach kingdom come to your students. It simply means that you should walk in that purpose. Your gift may be evident in the exceptional way you connect with your students. There may be something about the way you teach and inspire your students that stand out among your peers. People may come to you for advice. You allow your light to shine without having to proclaim loudly Who you represent. *"A man's gift makes room for him and brings him before the great."* [a] Using your gift and living in your purpose will place you in positions that will provide you a platform for winning others to Christ.

I used teaching as an example, but your gift doesn't have to be your vocation, although in many cases they are the same. Whatever gift God has given you should also be used to uplift and encourage those members of your local church. If you have the gift of teaching, consider volunteering to teach Children's Church, Sunday School, or assist others with reading or tutoring. If you've been blessed with the talent to play a musical instrument, perhaps you can participate in the church band or teach music lessons. Whatever the calling, the mission is the same—pointing others to Christ.

Maybe you're still wondering how managing your money and living your purpose are connected. Obviously, it takes money to do most anything, from paying your bills to buying things you need and saving for future needs. If you are not able to do these things due to lack of money, chances are you are not going to project a life of purpose. Going through life worrying about the amount of debt you're under, living paycheck to paycheck, or not having enough money to meet your needs cause you to stress. Financial stress can cause heart attacks, strokes, depression, and anxiety. Don't think because you're young that you're not susceptible to these illnesses. More frequently you hear about young people dying from heart attacks or committing suicide from depression.

When you don't manage your finances well, you deprive yourself of blessings. God loves it when you can freely give your time, talent and treasure and he responds accordingly. If your money is tied up in debt payments, it's going to be a challenge to be generous with your treasure. Your debt may drive you to get a second job that limits the amount of time you can give to others. Poorly managing your money does not allow you to focus on what matters. Your treasures will increase as your ability and opportunities to bless others increase. Don't allow debt, poor money management, and greed steal your blessings.

Many years ago, I lived in Indianapolis and worked for a military finance office. One of my coworkers tragically lost her seven-year old daughter when their home was blown up due to a malfunctioning furnace. The incident happened one week before Christmas. It was the saddest thing that had ever happened to someone I knew, and my heart ached for my coworker. It is common to collect money throughout the workplace to help coworkers who experience hardships like this one. As the envelope circulated, I overheard one coworker say to another, "I would give something but I just made my car payment, and I'm broke." This was coming from an individual who frequently shopped for the latest fashions, drove a luxury car, and took elaborate vacations. But, she was not able to bless this family with one dollar. Poor money management caused her to miss an opportunity to be a blessing to someone else. You don't ever want to be in this situation.

Blessing others doesn't necessarily mean that you must perform some great act of charity, or sacrifice all that you have. Blessing others is a matter of helping others as opportunities present themselves. You can help others by engaging in acts of kindness like the ones below:

- Volunteer at a homeless shelter or food bank

- Give money to help those who have lost their home

- Give money to support your church or a specific ministry

- Help senior citizens navigate difficult paperwork or assisting with computer skills

- Buy school supplies or uniforms for a disadvantaged student

- Volunteer in a youth mentoring program like Big Brothers Big Sisters of America

- Invite someone to dinner who may be struggling financially and offer encouragement

- Tutor a child

- Send a care package to a military member serving overseas

- Give your gently used clothes or household goods to charity or someone in need

- Gift your business products or services to someone who needs them but cannot afford to purchases them

- Visit with someone who has been sick for an extended period (call first)

- Share your home by hosting a group bible study, support group, or fun get-together

- Share your car by offering to drive others who do not have transportation to work, school, or church

These are just a few examples of how to bless others using the blessings that were generously given to you. Even though I don't deserve it, my life has been extremely blessed. I attribute God's favor to my willingness to yield to opportunities He places before me to help others. I encourage you to prepare your heart and mind to identify opportunities to be of service to others. When they come, don't look the other way. Be obedient to the Spirit's tug at your heart and respond accordingly. When your mind tries to tell you that you can't afford to give or that you don't have the time to help, push through those moments of doubt and trust that God will keep His word. *"Give, and it will be given to you. Good measure, pressed down, shaken together, running over, will be put into your lap. For with the measure you use it will be measured back to you.*[b] God has *always* provided and prospered my family and me, and I know he'll do the same for you when you bless others.

God wants to provide for you and to prosper you in every area of your life, whether it's your business, educational endeavors, recreation, health, marriage, and yes, your finances. *"Beloved, I wish above all things that thou mayest prosper and be in health, even as thy soul prospereth."*[c] Most people think of money when they hear the word, "prosper." Being prosperous doesn't mean having a certain salary. It has nothing to do with the amount of money you have. Being prosperous is simply being able to meet your needs and wants. It's freedom. Prosperity is being free from debt and stress so that you have the freedom to serve others. You are blessed to be a blessing. In turn, your kindness and generosity will point others to Christ. Everything you acquire and accomplish is by God's generous grace. It all belongs to Him. While others may be impressed with what you have, God is more concerned about what you *do* with what you have. Don't hoard your blessings. Use them to glorify God. That is the point of it all.

* * *

1. Which of the ten steps to becoming financially healthy do you find to be the most challenging? Why?

_____

_____

_____

_____

2. When was the last time you used your blessings to be a blessing to others?

_____

_____

_____

_____

_____

NOTES

Introduction

1. Richard Fry, "Millennials Overtake Baby Boomers as America's Largest Generation," Pew Research Center, April 25, 2016, **http://www.pewresearch.org/fact-tank/2016/04/25/millennials-overtake-baby-boomers/**, last accessed May 3, 2017

2. Jim Tankersley, "Baby Boomers are What's Wrong with America's Economy," *Washington Post,* November 5, 2015, **https://www.washingtonpost.com/posteverything/wp/2015/11/05/baby-boomers-are-whats-wrong-with-americas-economy/?utm_term=.7c0540336be8**, last accessed May 3, 2017.

Chapter 1

1. Mary Boweman, "Spending More on Coffee Than Investing?" *USA Today*, January 11, 2017, **http://www.usatoday.com/story/money/nation-now/2017/01/11/spending-more-coffee-than-investing-youre-not-alone/96385882/**, last accessed May 3, 2017

2. Council for Economic Education, "The 2016 National State of Financial and Economic Education," **http://www.surveyofthestates.com/#debt**, last accessed May 5, 2017

Chapter 2

1. Johnnie Dent Jr., Good Reads, **https://www.goodreads.com/quotes/7264408-an-excuse-is-the-most-expensive-brand-of-self-defeat**, last accessed May 3, 2017

2. John H, Fleming, "Millennials Most Likely to Shop for Fun, on Impulse," *Gallop Business Journal, May 26, 2016,* **http://www.gallup.com/businessjournal/191852/millennials-likely-shop-fun-impulse.aspx**, last accessed May 3, 2017

3. AICPA, American Institute of CPAs, "Saving is a Top Priority for Millennials, but Two-thirds Say Impulse Spending is a Major Barrier," Press Release, March 24, 2016, **https://www.aicpa.org/press/pressreleases/2016/pages/saving-is-a-top-priority-for-millennials.aspx**, last accessed May 5, 2017

4. Isrealmore Ayivor, Good Reads, **https://www.goodreads.com/quotes/search?utf8=%E2%9C%93&q=laziness+ayivor&commit=Search** last accessed May 3, 2017

5. National Center for Health Statistics, Life Expectancy, **https://www.cdc.gov/nchs/fastats/life-expectancy.htm, last accessed May 3, 2017**

6. Jane Hunt, *"Procrastination: Preventing the Decay of Delay,"* Aspire Press, 2015, p.32

7. Comparative Influence, *Oxford Reference*, Oxford University Press, 2017, **http://www.oxfordreference.com/view/10.1093/oi/authority.2011080309562863**, last accessed May 3, 2017

8. Dan Schawbel, "10 New Findings About the Millennial Consumer," *Forbes,* January 20, 2015, **http://www.forbes.com/sites/danschawbel/2015/01/20/10-new-findings-about-the-millennial-consumer/#46a8ce1a28a8**, last accessed May 3, 2017

9. Chris Brown, God's View: It's Okay to Have Nice Things! August 29, 2016, Stewardship, http:**//www.stewardship.com/articles/god-s-view-it-s-okay-to-have-nice-things**, last accessed May 3, 2017

Chapter 3

1. Nathaniel Popper, "How Millennials Became Spooked by Credit Cards," *The New York Times,* August 14, 2016, **http://www.nytimes.com/2016/08/15/business/dealbook/why-millennials-are-in-no-hurry-to-take-on-debt.html?_r=0**, last accessed May 5, 2017

2. Lindsay Konsko, "Your Employer Won't be Looking at your Credit Score, Here's Why," Nerdwallet, November 4, 2016, **https://www.nerdwallet.com/blog/finance/credit-score-employer-checking/**, last accessed May 3, 2017

3. Blain Lyerla, "What are the Different Credit Score Ranges," April 13, 2015, Experion, **http://www.experian.com/blogs/ask-experian/infographic-what-are-the-different-scoring-ranges/**, last accessed May 5, 2017

4. 360 Degrees of Financial Literacy, Understanding Your Credit Report, The American Institute of Certified Public Accountants, 2004-2017, **http://www.360financialliteracy.org/Topics/Credit-and-Debt/Credit-Cards/Advantages-and-Disadvantages-of-Credit-Cards**, last accessed May 3, 2017

5. Kathleen Elkins, "Mark Cuban: 'Don't Use Credit Cards,'" CNBC News, May 27, 2017, **http://www.msn.com/en-us/money/spendingandborrowing/mark-cuban-dont-use-credit-cards/ar-BBBywS9?li=BBnb4R7**, last accessed May 28

Chapter 4

1. Student Loan Hero, "A Look at the Shocking Student Loan Debt Statistics for 2017," **https://studentloanhero.com/student-loan-debt-statistics/**, last accessed May 3, 2017

2. J. Maureen Henderson, "The Scary Truth About Millennials and Student Loan Debt," *Forbes*, April 7, 2016, **http://www.forbes.com/sites/jmaureenhenderson/2016/04/07/the-scary-truth-about-millennials-and-student-loan-debt/#5f8ba87fb8ae**, last accessed May 3, 2017

3. Christina Counch, "What to do when you can't pay student loan," Bankrate, 2017, **http://www.bankrate.com/finance/college-finance/what-to-do-when-you-can-t-pay-student-loan-1.aspx#ixzz4JimcYRH8**, last accessed May 3, 2017

4. Federal Student Aid, Department of Education, "Don't get discouraged if you are in default on your federal student loan," **https://studentaid.ed.gov/sa/repay-loans/default/get-out#loan-repayment**, last accessed May 3, 2017

5. Indeed, **https://www.indeed.com/**, last accessed May 3, 2017

Chapter 5

1. Robert Harrow, "Average Credit Card Debt in America: 2016 Facts & Figures," ValuePenguin, **November 28, 2016, https://www.valuepenguin.com/average-credit-card-debt**, last accessed May 5, 2017

2. Nathaniel Popper, "How Millennials Became Spooked by Credit Cards," *The New York Times*, August 14, 2016, **https://www.nytimes.com/2016/08/15/business/dealbook/why-millennials-are-in-no-hurry-to-take-on-debt.html?_r=0** last accessed May 5, 2017

3. Bev O'Shae, "43% of Millennials Have Bad Credit, Transunion Says," Nerdwallet, May 9, 2016, **https://www.nerdwallet.com/blog/finance/millennials-have-bad-credit-transunion/**, last accessed May 5, 2017

4. Jeff Cox, "There Are More Payday Lenders in the U.S. Than McDonald's," NBC News, November 24, 2014, **http://www.nbcnews.com/business/economy/there-are-more-payday-lenders-u-s-mcdonalds-n255156**, last accessed May 5, 2017

5. Kristen Doerer, "Why are Millennials Turning to Payday Loans and Pawn Shops," PBS Newshour, January 29, 2016, **http://www.pbs.org/newshour/making-sense/why-are-millennials-turning-to-payday-loans-and-pawn-shops/**, last accessed May 5, 2017

6. Mandi Woodruff, "The $46 Billion Payday Lending Industry is in for a Big Blow," Yahoo Finance, February 10, 2016, **http://finance.yahoo.com/news/CFPB-payday-lending-rules-explained-192558796.html, last accessed May 5, 2017**

7. Consumer Financial Protection Bureau Proposes Rule to End Payday Debt Traps, Consumer Financial Protection Bureau, June 2, 2016, **http://www.consumerfinance.gov/about-us/newsroom/consumer-financial-protection-bureau-proposes-rule-end-payday-debt-traps/**, last accessed May 5, 2017

8. Brandon Cornett, "FHA vs. Conventional Mortgage Loan: Weighing Your Options," Home Buying Institute, 2016, **http://www.homebuyinginstitute.com/mortgagetypes_article6.php**, last accessed May 5, 2017

9. Trulia, "Buying a House? Here are 6 Reasons to Love A 20% Down Payment," *Forbes,* February 26, 2014, **http://www.forbes.com/sites/trulia/2014/02/26/buying-a-house-here-are-6-reasons-to-love-a-20-down-payment/#3bf338f654f6**, last accessed May 5, 2017

Chapter 6

1. Roxana Maddahi, "Talking Money Before Marriage," *Huffington Post*, February 16, 2017, **http://www.huffingtonpost.com/roxana-maddahi/talking-money-before-marriage_b_9212554.html**, last accessed May 5, 2017

2. New Release, "Survey Finds Many Couples Maintain Separate Bank Accounts," TD Bank, March 24, 2014, **https://mediaroom.tdbank.com/2014-03-24-TD-Bank-Survey-Finds-Many-Couples-Maintain-Separate-Bank-Accounts**, last accessed May 5, 2017

3. Dustin Riechmann, "Should Married Couples Have Joint or Separate Bank Accounts?" Engaged Marriage, 2017, **http://www.engagedmarriage.com/should-married-couples-have-joint-or-separate-bank-accounts/**, last accessed May 5, 2017

4. Casey Slide, "How to Deal with Financial Income Inequality in Marriage," Money Crashers, **http://www.moneycrashers.com/how-to-handle-income-inequality-in-marriage/** last accessed May 5, 2017

Chapter 7

1. Jane Hunt, Financial Freedom; How to Manage Your Money Wisely, Aspire Press, 2014, p29

2. Landon Dowdy, "Millennials are More Generous Than You Think, CNBC," December 8, 2015, **http://www.cnbc.com/2015/12/08/millennials-are-more-generous-than-you-think.html**, last accessed May 5, 2017

3. Ron Blue, "Eternal Perspective," Focus on the Family, **http://www.focusonthefamily.com/lifechallenges/managing-money/gods-big-ideas-about-finances/eternal-perspective**, last accessed May 5, 2017

4. Dr. Tony Evans, *"Living in Financial Victory,"* Moody Publishers, 2013, p15

Chapter 8

1. Suze Orman, *"The Money Book for the Young, Fabulous, and Broke,"* Penguin Group, 2005, p.146

2. Baynote, BCGPerspectives, "Buy Buy Birdie," **http://www.baynote.com/wp-content/uploads/2013/01/Baynote_BuyBuyBirdie_Infographic. png**, last accessed May 5, 2017

Chapter 9

1. Cost Helper Health, "How Much Does a Broken Arm Cost?" **http://health.costhelper.com/broken-arm.html, last accessed May 5, 2017**

2. Cost Helper, How Much Does an Appendectomy Costs? **http://health.costhelper.com/appendicitis.html**, last accessed May 5, 2017

3. Mary Bowerman, "Spending More on Coffee Than Investing? You're not alone," *USA Today Network*, January 11, 2017, **http://www.usatoday.com/story/money/nation-now/2017/01/11/spending-more-coffee-than-investing-youre-not-alone/96385882/,** last accessed May 5, 2017

4. Catherine Collinson, "Millennial Workers: An Emerging Generation of Super Savers," The 15th Annual Transamerica Retirement Survey conducted by the Transamerica Center for Retirement Studies, April 2015, **https://www.transamericacenter.org/docs/default-source/resources/center-research/tcrs2014_sr_millennials.pdf,** last accessed May 5, 2017

5. Zero Based Budget, **http://www.zerobasedbudgethq.com/templates**, last accessed May 5, 2017

SCRIPTURE REFERENCES

Unless otherwise noted, all scripture is from Bible Gateway, English Standard Version, www.biblegateway.com.

Introduction
a. 2 Chronicles 1:10
b. Proverbs 4:7 (KJV)
c. Matthew 25:23
d. James 1:5
e. Proverbs 19:20

Chapter 1
Romans 12:2

Chapter 2
a. Proverbs 21:5
b. Jeremiah 29:11
c. Psalms 90:12
d. Ecclesiastes 9:10
e. Ecclesiastes 11:4
f. 2 Timothy 1:7
g. Ecclesiastes 10:18
h. Proverbs 20:4
i. Proverbs 13:4
j. Proverbs 22:1
k. Proverbs 13:7
l. Psalms 139:13-14
m. Philippians 4:12-13

Chapter 3
a. Proverbs 22:3

b. James 4:13-14

c. Proverbs 22:7

Chapter 4
a. Proverbs 6:5

Chapter 5
a. Ecclesiastes 5:4-5

b. Luke 14:28

c. Proverbs 3:5

d. Proverbs 16:3

e. 2 Corinthians 9:6-7

Chapter 6
a. Ecclesiastes 4:9-10

b. Genesis 2:24

c. Philippians 2:3-4

d. Ephesians 5:22-28

e. Proverbs 22:6

Chapter 7
a. Ecclesiastes 5:10

b. Psalms 24:1

c. Matthew 25:29

d. 2 Corinthians 9:10-14

e. 2 Corinthians 9:6-7

f. 3 John 2

g. Matthew 6:19-20

Chapter 8
a. Proverbs 27:23
b. 1 Samuel 16:7

Chapter 9
a. 3 John 2
b. Matthew 5:42
c. Galatians 6:9

Chapter 10
a. Proverbs 18:16
b. Luke 6:38
c. Proverbs 11:25 (KJV)

Recommended Reading

- *The Total Money Makeover*, Dave Ramsey, Thomas Nelson Publisher, Nashville, Tennessee, 2013

- *30 Days to Taming Your Finances: What to Do (and Not Do) to Better Manage Your Money*, Deborah Smith Pegues, Harvest House Publishers, Eugene, Oregon, 2006

- *Retired Inspired*, Chris Hogan, Ramsey Press, Brentwood, Tennessee, 2016

- *The Spender's Guide to Debt-Free Living,* Anna Newell Jones, HarperCollins Publishers, Broadway, New York, NY, 2016

- *The Wealth Cure: Putting Money in its Place,* Hill Harper, Penguin Random House, New York, New York, 2011

- *The Solomon Secret: Financial Wisdom from King Solomon,* History's Wealthiest Man, Bruce Fleet, Penguin Group, New York, New York, 2010

www.ingramcontent.com/pod-product-compliance
Lightning Source LLC
Chambersburg PA
CBHW060007210326
41520CB00009B/854